The Bush Theatre presents
the world premiere of

Little Platoons

by Steve Waters

19 January – 19 February 2011

The Bush Theatre would like to give particular thanks to:
aka, Jason King and Pieter Strombeck at Land Securities,
MacColl Media Ltd, Sarah Peachey, M.A.C. Cosmetics
and the staff at St Paul's School

Cast and Creative Team

Brandon	**Joe Cole**
Marcus	**Kerron Darby**
Sadie	**Holli Dempsey**
Amitha	**Mandeep Dhillon**
Sam	**Otto Farrant**
Polly	**Joanne Froggatt**
Lara	**Susannah Harker**
Martin	**Richard Henders**
Rachel	**Claire Price**
Parvez	**Christopher Simpson**
Nick	**Andrew Woodall**
Director	**Nathan Curry**
Designer	**Signe Beckmann**
Lighting Designer	**Mark Doubleday**
Sound Designer	**Tom Gibbons**
Assistant Director	**Chanya Button**
Assistant Designer / Wardrobe Supervisor	**Thomasin Marshall**
Deputy Production Manager	**Ben Ainsley**
Deputy Stage Manager	**Mary Hely**
Assistant Stage Manager (placement)	**Nikki Radford**
Props Assistant	**Adam McElderry**
Costume Buyer	**Amy Cook**
Set Builder	**Dave Larking**

Joe Cole Brandon

Theatre includes: *Polling Booth* (Theatre503); *Relish* (National Youth Theatre); *Brixton Rock* (Young Vic); *Talking to Byron* (National Youth Theatre/ Roundhouse); *Tits and Teeth* (National Youth Theatre/Soho); *Laters* (Drill Hall).

TV includes: *Injustice, Come Fly with Me, Citizen Shane, Stanley Park, The Bill, Holby City, Concrete Jungle.*

Film includes: *Hand, Assessment.*

Kerron Darby Marcus

Kerron trained at the Identity Drama School, the United Kingdom's first black drama school.

Theatre includes: *Totally Over You* (Arcola); *Gunshot* (Stratford Circus).

TV includes: *The Bill, Casualty, Beautiful People, Silent Witness.*

Film includes: *Top Girl, Scouting for Rude Boys, God's View.*

Holli Dempsey Sadie

Theatre includes: *Make Love Not War* (Talawa); *No Way Home* (Made in Da Shade); *Our Baby Charlie* (Theatre Royal Stratford); *Reparations* (Black History tour); *The Final Hour* (Breaking Walls).

TV includes: *Tracey Beaker, The Bill.*

Film includes: *Dots, The Fighter's Ballad, Game Keepers Without Games.*

Mandeep Dhillon Amitha

Mandeep trained at the Harris Drama School.

Theatre includes: *The Tempest, Life* (Candi Productions); *New Path, Twisted Minds* (Fearnhill Productions); *Oliver, Annie* (Wilbury Productions).

Film includes: *Some Dogs Bite.*

Otto Farrant Sam

Otto is currently training at Stagecoach Theatre School, Battersea.

Theatre includes: *The Habit of Art, Oedipus* (National); *The Merry Wives of Windsor* (Shakespeare's Globe).

TV includes: *The Bill.*

Film includes: *Salmon Fishing in the Yemen, The Great Ghost Rescue, Clash of the Titans, Handgum, Panic, Happy Ever After.*

Joanne Froggatt Polly

Theatre includes: *All About My Mother* (Old Vic); *Who's Afraid of Virginia Woolf?* (Royal Exchange); *Playhouse Creatures* (West Yorkshire Playhouse); *Be My Baby* (Soho).

TV includes: *Downton Abbey, Identity, Moving On, The Butterfly Effect, Murder in the Outback, Rebus, The Street, See No Evil, Life on Mars, Missing, Island at War, Danielle Cable: Eye Witness, Nature Boy, Outside In, Other People's Children, Paradise Heights, Stretford Wives, The Last Detective, Lorna Doone, A Touch of Frost, Dinner Ladies, Coronation Street.*

Film includes: *In Our Name, Echoes, Miranda.*

Susannah Harker Lara

Theatre includes: *A Good Death* (National Theatre Studio); *Lucky Seven, The Debutante Ball* (Hampstead); *Jingo: A Farce of War* (Finborough); *On the Shore of the Wide World* (Royal Exchange/National); *Three Sisters* (Playhouse); *The Little Black Book* (Riverside Studios); *The Browning Version* (Derby Playhouse); *Uncle Vanya* (Gate, London/New York); *Tartuffe* (Almeida); *The Importance of Being Earnest* (Aldwych); *She Stoops to Conquer, Venus Observed, Coriolanus* (Chichester Festival); *Racing Demon* (National); *Look Back in Anger* (Bristol Old Vic).

TV includes: *Moving On, Midsomer Murders, Perfect Parents, Waking the Dead, Murder in Mind, Ultra-Violet, Under the Sun, Pride and Prejudice, Faith, The Memoirs of Sherlock Holmes, Adam Bede, House of Cards, Chancer, Till we Meet Again, The Fear, Troubles, The Lady's Not for Burning.*

Film includes: *My Mother* (short film), *The Calling, Trance, Intimacy, Burke and Wills, White Mischief, A Dry White Season, The Crucifier of Blood, Surviving Picasso.*

Richard Henders Martin

Theatre for the Bush includes: *Kiss the Sky.*

Other theatre includes: *Lord of the Rings* (Theatre Royal Drury Lane); *The Seagull* (Bristol Old Vic); *Rookery Nook* (Oxford Stage Company); *Pacific Overtures* (Donmar Warehouse, Olivier Award nomination); *The White Guard, Love's Labour's Lost, Anything Goes, The Cherry Orchard, Summerfolk, The Merchant of Venice, Candide, Caroline, Or Change* (National); *Alice in Wonderland* (RSC); *Three Sisters* (Chichester Festival); *Oh! What A Lovely War* (National tour/ Roundhouse); *Frogs* (National/tour); *The Knocky* (Royal Court); *An Absolute Turkey* (Leatherhead/West End); *Hallisinia* (National/Tate Gallery); *A Tribute to the Blues Brothers* (UK tour); *As You Like It* (Cheek by Jowl/world tour); *Just So* (Tricycle); *Macbeth* (Royal Exchange); *Stolen Christmas, Secrets of Theodore Brown* (Unicorn); *Cutters Story* (Avignon International Festival); *Julius Caesar* (Birmingham Rep); *The Warehouse,The Cherry Blossom Tree* (Liverpool Playhouse); *London by Lamplight* (Polka); *Captain Swing* (Leeds Playhouse).

TV includes: *Kingdom, Inspector Lynley Mysteries, Foyle's War, The Children of the New Forest, Pie in the Sky, Can You Hear Me Thinking, Brother Cadfael, The Chronicles of Narnia, Oranges Are Not the Only Fruit, Brookside.*

Film includes: *Pork Steak, The Merchant of Venice, Vroom, A Night With a Woman, A Day With Charlie.*

Claire Price Rachel

Theatre includes: *A Midsummer Night's Dream, Love in a Wood* (New End, Hampstead); *The Dark Room* (Finborough); *The Giant Prince* (Quiksilver Children's Theatre tour); *Dead White Males* (Nuffield); *When Did You Last See My Mother* (BAC); *Hard Times* (The Good Company); *Ursula* (The Wrestling School); *Volpone, Don Carlos* (RSC); *As You Like It* (Manchester Royal Exchange); *Twelfth Night* (Liverpool Playhouse); *Cyrano, The Power of Yes, The Relapse* (National); *Mean Tears, Richard III, Much Ado About Nothing* (Sheffield Crucible); *The Tempest* (Sheffield Crucible/Old Vic); *Brand* (RSC/ Haymarket); *Dr Faustus* (Bristol Old Vic); *Lady From the Sea* (Birmingham Rep); *The White Devil* (Menier Chocolate Factory); *Private Lives* (Hampstead); *Mary Stuart* (Theatre Clwyd, winner of the TMA Award).

TV includes: *London's Burning, The Knock, Whistleblower, Murder in Mind, Midsomer Murders, Twelfth Night, Poirot: The Hollow, Rebus, Dalziel and Pascoe, Apparitions.*

Film includes: *Hereafter, Cuckoo, Solo Shuttle.*

Christopher Simpson Parvez

Theatre includes: *Fallujah* (Truman Brewery); *The Bacchae of Baghdad* (Abbey, Dublin); *Pericles* (RSC/Cardboard Citizens); *The Ramayana* (National); *Fragile Land* (Hampstead).

TV includes: *Spooks: Code 9, White Teeth, Second Generation, State of Play.*

Forthcoming films include the Cuban-set drama *The Day of the Flowers* (directed by John Roberts) and Mira Fornayová's psychological drama *Little Foxes*.

Other film work includes: *Brick Lane*, *Mischief Night*, *Code 46*, *The Ground Beneath Her Feet*, *Le Fils De Mon Pere*.

Christoper has written a song cycle, *Very Present Tense*, which premiered during the Liverpool Capital of Culture and another documentary for BBC Radio 4 called *Other*.

Andrew Woodall Nick

Theatre includes: *Hedda Gabler* (Gate, Dublin); *Much Ado About Nothing*, *The Voysey Inheritance*, *The Life of Galileo*, *Luther*, *The Shape of the Table*, *Racing Demon*, *Women Beware Women* (National); *Gaslight*, *King Lear*, *The Provok'd Wife*, *Cloud Nine*, *Waste* (Old Vic); *As You Like It* (Wyndhams); *As You Desire Me* (Playhouse); *The Sugar Syndrome*, *Disappeared*, *Search and Destroy*, *Weldon Rising* (Royal Court); *Burning Issues* (Hampstead); *Certain Young Men*, *Butterfly Kiss* (Almeida); *A Letter of Resignation* (Savoy); *Our Late Night* (Ambassadors); *Don Carlos* (Glasgow Citizens); *Vieux Carre* (Nottingham Playhouse); *The Art of Success* (Paines Plough).

TV includes: *The Suspicions of Mr Whicher*, *Above Suspicion*, *Personal Affairs*, *Men are Wonderful*, *Place of Execution*, *Heartbeat*, *Lawless*, *Hear the Silence*, *Charles II*, *Starhunter*, *Ultimate Force*, *Dalziel and Pascoe*, *Murder Rooms*, *Hearts and Bones*, *Harbour Lights*, *Gimme Gimme Gimme*, *Nature Boy*, *Kavanagh QC*, *Degrees of Error*, *Seaforth*, *Headhunters*, *Prime Suspect III*, *Between the Lines*, *Underbelly*, *Wish Me Luck* and *Hannay*.

Film includes: *Hypnotic*, *The Count of Monte Cristo*, *Regeneration*, *Johnny English Reborn*.

Signe Beckmann (Designer)

Signe is from Denmark, Copenhagen and trained at the Danish Design School and the Motley Theatre Design Course.

Theatre includes: *Tales of the Harrow Road* (Soho); *Some Voices, A Prayer for Owen Meany, The Mill on the Floss* (LAMDA); *Kain* (NyAveny and tour); *Dr Faustus* (Watford Palace); *House of Bernarda Alba, Dealer's Choice* (Embassy); *Ghosts* (Young Vic); *King Ubu* (Takkelloftet, Royal Danish Opera House and tour); *Blackbird, Sexual Perversity in Chicago* (Norwich Playhouse); *About Tommy, Plasticine* (Southwark Playhouse); *Dancing at Lughnasa* (Aubade Hall, Japan); *Scenes from an Execution* (Hackney Empire); *Pedro and the Captain* (Arcola); *Love in Idleness* (Bristol Old Vic); *Breaking News* (Theatre 503).

Opera includes: *La Serva Padrona* (Sa de Miranda, Portugal); *Volume* (ENO Opera Works); *Eugene Onegin, Giasone* (Iford Arts).

Dance and circus credits include: *Meridian, Phantasy* (Rambert, Queen Elizabeth Hall); *Santa's Shadow* (Dansehallerne); *A Night For One* (European tour).

Signe was also stylist on *Kate Moss Liberation* (Liberation Magazine).

Chanya Button (Assistant Director)

Chanya has a BA in English Language and Literature from Oxford University, and an MA in Theatre Directing from RADA, from which she graduated in 2010. Chanya has also worked in script development at Warner Brothers and the UK Film Council, and as an Assistant Director in Film, most recently on *Harry Potter and the Deathly Hallows*.

Theatre as a Director includes: *Victory at the Dirt Palace, Inglourious Basterds* (RADA); *The Rivals* (Oxford Playhouse); *Angels in America: Millenium Approaches* (Oxford Union Debating Chamber); *Arcadia* (UK tour and Bedlam Theatre, Edinburgh); *Hamlet* (Old Fire Station Theatre, Oxford); *Switch Triptych* (Burton Taylor Theatre, Oxford), and Assistant Director for *Broken Glass* (Tricycle).

Nathan Curry (Director)

Nathan joined the Bush as a Creative Associate in 2008 and directed *Bufonidae* by Bryony Lavery as part of the Broken Space Season. He became an Associate Director in February 2010.

Nathan is also the Artistic Director of the award-winning ensemble tangled feet. For tangled feet Nathan has directed: *The Measurement Shop, The Cells* (with Theatre Venture); *Wishful* (with EEA); *Home, I Confess, Game? Emily's Kitchen, Lost Property* and *Catching Dust*. tangled feet's new show, *All That is Solid Melts into Air* will premiere at the G+D International Festival in July 2011.

Other directing credits include: *As You Were* (Edinburgh Fringe Festival); *One Mile Away* (promenade performance in Elephant and Castle); *Fixer* (HighTide Festival), *Romeo and Juliet* (New Wimbledon Studio); *Weapons of Happiness* (Finborough); *Ya Get Me?* (for the Old Vic Education Department). Nathan also developed *Movieplex*, an interactive outdoor experience with the National Theatre Studio and Nutkhut Theatre Company.

Nathan was the Assistant Director on *A Moon for the Misbegotten* (Broadway and the Old Vic) and was Staff Director at the National Theatre on *The Life of Galileo*, both assisting Howard Davies.

Nathan trained at Middlesex University and subsequently has received training from the National Theatre Studio Directors' Course, Katie Mitchell Directors' Course, the Royal Shakespeare Company (with Cicely Berry) and the Stary Theatre, Krakow.

Mark Doubleday (Lighting Designer)

Mark has lit over two hundred and fifty productions in most UK theatres and also New York, Washington, Europe and Asia.

Theatre for the Bush includes: *Elling*, *The Danny Crowe Show*.

Recent work includes: *Behzti* (Birmingham Rep); *Lysistrata* (Houston Grand Opera/NewYork City Opera); *Hansel and Gretel* (Scottish Opera); *Love's Labour's Lost* (Washington DC Shakespeare Theatre and RSC); *Tannhäuser* (Los Angeles Opera); *The Mikado*, *Iolanthe*, *The Pirates of Penzance* (Gielgud Theatre, West End); *Familyman* (Theatre Royal, Stratford East); *The Cunning Little Vixen* (La Finta Giardiniera); *A Midsummer Night's Dream* (RCM); *The Cumner Affair*, *Salad Days* (Tête à Tête); *Tannhäuser* (Teatro Real, Madrid); *Le Nozze di Figaro* (Los Angeles Opera).

Tom Gibbons (Sound Designer)

Tom trained at Central School of Speech and Drama in Theatre Sound and is resident sound designer for the international physical theatre company Parrot {in the} Tank.

Theatre for the Bush includes: *50 Ways to Leave Your Lover*, *50 Ways to Leave Your Lover at Christmas*, *Broken Space Season* (Associate Sound Designer).

Recent design credits for Parrot include: *Excursions* (Arts Depot and Roundhouse); *Just Above the Below* (Arts Theatre, Paradise Gardens Festival, tour of Slovakia); *Freeman Gallop* (ICA London, Prague Scenofest, Budva Montenegro); *Storm in a Teacup* (Arts Depot).

Other theatre design credits include: *The Chairs* (Theatre Royal Bath); *The Country*, *The Road to Mecca*, *The Roman Bath*, *1936*, *The Shawl* (Arcola); *Everything Must Go*, *Soho Streets* (Soho); *Holes* (New Wimbledon Studio); *Terror Tales* (Hampstead Studio); *The Hostage*,

Present Tense (Southwark Playhouse); *Faustus* (Watford Palace and tour); *Faithless Bitches* (Courtyard); *FAT* (Oval House); *Just Me Bell* (Graeae, tour); *Blue Heaven* (Finborough); *Pitching In* (Latitude Festival and tour); *Overspill, The Shape of Things, The Old Man and the Sea, This Limetree Bower, Someone Who'll Watch Over Me* (Cockpit); *US Love Bites* (Old Red Lion, Tristan Bates); *I Can Sing a Rainbow* with Nabokov and Sheffield Theatres (Lyceum Sheffield); *Pendulum* (Jermyn Street); *Journalist and Hope* (ICA London); *Machinal* (Central); *Bar of Ideas* (Paradise Gardens Festival and Glastonbury/Shangri-La).

Thomasin Marshall (Assistant Designer/Wardrobe Supervisor)

Thomasin recently trained at Motley. As well as designing, she is a freelance scenic painter and has worked as a creative workshop leader and design mentor employed by youth theatre groups.

Her recent design credits include: *Serendip* (Bike Shed Theatre, Exeter); *Henry IV Part One* (Drum Theatre, Plymouth); *Voyage to Change the World* (Design Mentor, Barbican Theatre, Plymouth); *The Misanthrope* (Drum Theatre, Plymouth); *The Hidden City Festival* (various site-specific venues, Part Exchange Co.); *One Small Step One Giant Leap* (site-specific promenade production, assistant designer to Nat Tarrab, Royal William Yard, Plymouth).

Steve Waters (Writer)

Theatre for the Bush includes: *The Contingency Plan* (*On the Beach* and *Resilience*) which was shortlisted for the 2009 John Whiting Award and subsequently adapted and broadcast by BBC Radio 3.

Other writing for theatre includes: *Fast Labour* (Hampstead in association with West Yorkshire Playhouse); *Out of Your Knowledge* (Menagerie Theatre, Pleasance, Edinburgh/East Anglian tour); *World Music* (Sheffield Crucible and subsequent transfer to the Donmar Warehouse); *The Unthinkable* (Sheffield Crucible); *English Journeys, After the Gods* (Hampstead); a translation/adaptation of a new play by Philippe Minyana, *Habitats* (Gate, London/Tron, Glasgow); *Flight Without End* (LAMDA).

Writing for TV and radio includes: *Safe House* (BBC4); *The Moderniser* (BBC R4). Steve is currently writing a film version of *The Contingency Plan* (Cowboy Films/Film4).

Steve runs the Birmingham MPhil in Playwriting, and is a member of the British Theatre Consortium. He is the author of *The Secret Life of Plays*, published by Nick Hern Books.

The Bush Theatre

'One of the most experienced prospectors of raw talent in Europe'
The Independent

Since its inception in 1972, the Bush Theatre has pursued its singular vision of discovery, risk and entertainment from its home on the corner of Shepherds Bush Green. That vision is valued and embraced by a community of audience and artists radiating out from our distinctive corner of West London across the world. The Bush is a local theatre with an international reputation. From its beginning, the Bush has produced hundreds of groundbreaking premieres, many of them Bush commissions, and hosted guest productions by leading companies and artists from across the world. On any given night, those queuing at the foot of our stairs to take their seats could have travelled from Auckland or popped in from round the corner.

What draws them to the Bush is the promise of a good night out and our proven commitment to launch, from our stage, successive generations of playwrights and artists. Samuel Adamson, David Eldridge, Jonathan Harvey, Catherine Johnson, Tony Kushner, Stephen Poliakoff, Jack Thorne and Victoria Wood (all then unknown) began their careers at the Bush. The unwritten contract between talent and risk is understood by actors who work at the Bush, creating roles in untested new plays. Unique amongst local theatres, the Bush consistently draws actors of the highest reputation and calibre. Joseph Fiennes and Ian Hart recently took leading roles in a first play by an unknown playwright to great critical success. John Simm and Richard Wilson acted in premieres both of which transferred into the West End. The Bush has won over 100 awards, and developed an enviable reputation for touring its acclaimed productions nationally and internationally.

Audiences and organisations far beyond our stage profit from the risks we take. The value attached to the Bush by other theatres and by the film and television industries is both significant and considerable. The Bush receives more than 2,000 scripts every year, and reads and responds to them all. This is one small part of a comprehensive playwrights' development programme which nurtures the relationship between writer and director, as well as playwright residencies and commissions. Everything that we do to develop playwrights focuses them towards a production on our stage or beyond.

We have also launched an ambitious new education, training and professional development programme, bushfutures, providing opportunities for different sectors of the community and professionals to access the expertise of Bush playwrights, directors, designers, technicians and actors, and to play an active role in influencing the future development of the theatre and its programme. 2009 saw the launch of our new social networking and online publishing website www.bushgreen.org. The site is a great new forum for playwrights and theatre people to meet, share experiences and collaborate. Through this pioneering work, the Bush will reach and connect with new writers and new audiences, and find new plays to stage.

Josie Rourke, Artistic Director

At the Bush

We're a full-time staff of twelve, supported by a big team of associates, interns and freelancers. For ways to get involved please visit our website www.bushtheatre.co.uk/about/

Artistic Director	**Josie Rourke**
Executive Director	**Angela Bond**
Development Director	**Trish Wadley**
Box Office & Front of House Manager	**Annette Butler**
Marketing Manager	**Sophie Coke-Steel**
Producer	**Caroline Dyott**
Technical Manager	**Neil Hobbs**
Literary Administrator	**Naia Johns**
Development Manager	**Bethany Ann McDonald**
Theatre Administrator	**Francesca Miller**
Production Manager	**Anthony Newton**
Associate Director **bush**futures	**Anthea Williams**
Development Officer	Leonora Twynam
Associate Directors	Nathan Curry
	Charlotte Gwimmer
Pearson Writer-in-Residence	Nick Payne**
Composer on Attachment	Michael Bruce
Apprentice	Sade Banks
bushfutures Intern	Stacey Coyne
Press Representative	Kate Morley
Press Assistant	Charlotte Vikstrom
Bush Intern	Tamara Cowan
Leverhulme Trust Associate Playwright	Tom Wells
Creative Associates	Alice Lacey, Nessah Muthy, Ed Viney, Oliver Hawes, Kate Budgen, Hannah Dickinson
Associate Artists	Tanya Burns, Arthur Darvill, Chloe Emmerson, James Farncombe, Richard Jordan, Emma Laxton, Paul Miller, Lucy Osborne
Box Office Assistants	Chrissy Angus, Sade Banks, Nick Blakeley
Front of House Duty Managers	Kirsty Cox, Alex Hern, Lucy McCann, Kate McGregor, Ava Jade Morgan, Kirsty Patrick Ward
Duty Technicians	Ben Ainsley, Ruth Perrin, Adam McElderry

Bold indicates full-time stafff, regular indicates part-time/temporary
** Sponsored by the Peggy Ramsay Foundation Award as a part of the Pearson Playwrights' Scheme

The Bush Theatre
Shepherds Bush Green
London W12 8QD

Box Office: 020 8743 5050
www.bushtheatre.co.uk

The Alternative Theatre Company Ltd. (The Bush Theatre) is a Registered Charity number: 270080
Co. registration number 1221968 | VAT no. 228 3163 73

Supported by
ARTS COUNCIL ENGLAND

Be there at the beginning

The Bush Theatre would like to say a very special 'Thank You' to the following supporters, corporate sponsors and trusts and foundations, whose valuable contributions continue to help us nurture, develop and present some of the brightest new literary stars and theatre artists.

If you are interested in finding out how to be involved, visit the 'Support Us' section of our website, email development@bushtheatre.co.uk or call 020 8743 3584.

Bush Green

The Bush Theatre has recently launched **bushgreen**, a social networking website for people in theatre to connect, collaborate and publish plays in innovative ways. The mission of **bushgreen** is to connect playwrights with theatre practitioners and plays with producers to promote best practice and inspire the creation of exciting new theatre.

bushgreen allows members to:

- Submit plays directly to the Bush for our team to read and consider for production
- Connect with other writers, directors, producers and theatres
- Publish scripts online so more people can access your work
- Purchase scripts from hundreds of new playwrights

There are thousands of members and hundreds of plays on the site.

To join, log on to www.bushgreen.org

Bush Theatre Greening

The Bush Theatre is committed to greening itself to improve its environmental sustainability and reduce its carbon emissions.

We are doing this through a variety of practices including:

- Reducing materials by reusing and recycling all parts of our sets
- Keeping all props and costume for reuse and loan to other productions
- Looking carefully at the green credentials of all our suppliers

Our recent production of Anthony Weigh's play *Like a Fishbone* used a lighting rig which consumed approximately 64% less electricity than the previous production. Around 90% of the set of *The Aliens*, the first show in our Autumn/Winter 2010 Season, consisted of materials which were recycled from previous productions or sourced from reclamation yards.

The Bush is one of the first venues to be working with the Theatre's Trust ECOVENUE programme. The project provides specialist environmental advice and works with venues to create and develop environmental policies, offering assistance in monitoring energy, water use and waste diversion and procurement.

We are also working with the brilliant Julie's Bicycle (www.juliesbicycle.com) to develop schemes that green our work and to share these initiatives with other London theatres.

Why not help us expand this work by making a donation to the Bush? For more information visit www.bushtheatre.co.uk/support/

CLOSE-UP MAGIC: 40 years at the Bush Theatre

The Bush is making a book and it needs your help!

The Bush is delighted to be working with Third Millennium Publishing to create a magnificent, illustrated book to celebrate our 40th Anniversary in 2012.

CLOSE-UP MAGIC: 40 Years at the Bush Theatre will capture the glorious history of the Bush and we need your help to bring it to life. If you've got stories, photographs, or anything in between which might help us illuminate the Bush, please send us your contributions online at www.bushtheatrebook.com. Or you can send them by post to Neil Burkey, Editor, 40 Years at the Bush Theatre, Third Millennium Publishing, 2–5 Benjamin Street, London EC1M 5QL.

Early Bird Subscription Offer

Place your order by 28 February 2011 to guarantee your name in the book as a subscriber at a special early bird price.

The book will be published in September 2011, but by subscribing now you can benefit from a special price of £27.50 + p&p (the subscription price will go up to £35 + p&p 1 March 2011) – and have your name listed in the book itself as a subscriber.

To subscribe, please call Third Millennium Publishing on 020 7366 0144 or visit www.bushtheatrebook.com.

LITTLE PLATOONS

Steve Waters

*'If only I had the money, I'd start a school myself
where things would be run differently'*

Petra in Ibsen's An Enemy of the People

*'To love the little platoon that we belong to is the first link
in the series from which we proceed towards a love
of our country and mankind'*

*Edmund Burke,
'Observations on the Present State of the Nation'*

Characters

RACHEL DE WITT, *early forties, music teacher, white*
SAM, *twelve, her son, white*
MARTIN, *forties, Rachel's ex-partner, white*

NICK ORME, *late forties, setting up a free school, white*
LARA ORME, *his wife, early forties, likewise, white*
PARVEZ AKHTAR, *thirties, website designer, British Asian*

POLLY TYNEHAM, *twenties, Civil Servant at the Department
  for Education, white*

MARCUS, *a boy of fifteen, Afro-Caribbean*
AMITHA, *a girl of fifteen, British Asian*
SADIE, *a girl of fifteen, white*
BRANDON, *a boy of fifteen, white*

Settings

ACT ONE, EARLY AUGUST 2010
Rachel's house in Shepherd's Bush
Nick and Lara's house, also in Shepherd's Bush
A pub in Shepherd's Bush
Rachel's house
A meeting room in the Department of Education

ACT TWO, FEBRUARY 2011
A shop unit in West12 Shopping Centre, Shepherd's Bush

Author's Note

The following people have helped with the development of this play, but are not responsible for the views expressed within it:

Benz Adeyemi, Justin Althaus, Farhana Ahmed, Sade Banks, Smita Bora at Westminster Academy, Nathan Curry, Judy and David Dangoor, Rebecca Fortnum, Emma Garth, Nadine Gray, Lucy Heller, Jean Ketter, Corey McMahon, Caroline Prior, Professor Diane Reay, Josie Rourke, Kate Stratton, Grace Surrey, Anastasia de Waal, Susan Wokoma, Rachel Wolf, James Woods, Toby Young, all the teachers and parents who attended the Bush's focus group, the cast of the first production.

This play is dedicated to my friends and former colleagues Jon Blundell, Mandy Bolster, John Campbell, Nick Froy, Emma Garth, Keith and Jo Geary, Suzanne Marston, John Parry, Karen Reader, Mary Scott, Simon Smith, Jane Stanley, Bridie Sullivan, Pam Walkinshaw, Simon Veness, Chris Walters, Jean Welsh, and all the other teachers who labour away in state education.

This text went to press before the end of rehearsals and so may differ slightly from the play as performed.

ACT ONE

Scene One

RACHEL*'s house, early August, early afternoon. A spare, attractive room, with all the conventional middle-class accoutrements – stripped-pine floor, bare walls with one or two prints, a discreet television, barely visible, a window suggesting a small garden with a tree.* MARTIN *is sorting through a box full of books.* RACHEL *is painting a door a colour called 'scarab'.*

MARTIN. '*The State We're In.*'

'*The World We're In.*'

'*The Unfinished Revolution*'. '*Age Concern*'?

RACHEL. Not in the slightest bit bothered.

So what was the deal with Jo?

MARTIN. Er, not at liberty to say.

RACHEL. Okay. So she's out then?

MARTIN. Access Officers are not front line.

You're ring-fenced, of course. Teaching is ring-fenced.

Okay, '*Age Concern*'.

RACHEL. For now. Poor old Jo. Never mind, she was having a breakdown anyway. Easier to have a bloody good breakdown when you're freelance.

MARTIN. No one's out of the frame, Rach. All of us, one by one, had to justify our jobs to the senior team. Could we be outsourced? Guy in Bereavement Services suggested, I think ironically, maybe the public could self-cremate. I had it minuted that senior execs were exempt from their own fucking process.

RACHEL. Ooh, stunning career move, Marty.

MARTIN. One after the other. Family Support Team. Environmental Health. Housing. Like a balloon debate. I mean, did we vote for this, Rach?

RACHEL. Well, you, I think, voted Lib Dem.

MARTIN. Tactically! To keep these fuckers out.

I tell you what, if this is Compassionate Conservatism I'd hate to see the Dispassionate version.

Okay: Alistair Campbell's diaries.

Chris Mullin's diaries.

Alan Clark's diaries.

RACHEL. As in philandering Tory shit Alan Clark?

MARTIN. The same.

RACHEL. I'll have that.

MARTIN. Right. Okay. Actually, Dad bought me that.

RACHEL. How well he knew you.

MARTIN. By the way, what *is* that muck?

RACHEL. 'Scarab.'

MARTIN. 'Scarab.' It'll make the room darker.

RACHEL. That's the idea. As a sort of metaphor. Like the inky stuff squids squirt into the eyes of predators.

MARTIN. Cuttlefish do that. Not squids.

RACHEL. Cuttlefish are squids round here.

MARTIN *stands with the book, places it lamely on the floor.*

Sam's taking his time.

MARTIN. Adrift in the Westfield.

RACHEL. He's obsessed with that place.

MARTIN. He told me about his dream, his recurring dream.

RACHEL. Oh. He told you about that?

MARTIN. About that chavvy boy – Jordan, is it?

RACHEL. Brandon actually. I thought we thought 'chav' was a term that demonised the white working classes.

MARTIN. His word.

RACHEL. Dreams like that always come in the summer holidays. I get them too. He's readying himself.

MARTIN. I get the impression he's actually really scared about it, Rach.

Pause. RACHEL *stops painting.*

RACHEL. Ah, okay, fine, you, so you want to rehearse that again, stir it all up again?

MARTIN. I think – maybe we should think – yes. Think again. Maybe there are other options.

RACHEL. 'Think again.' Hang on, hang on, is this what you're saying now?

MARTIN. I think you'll find I always said that, always –

RACHEL. Hang on – I'm not hearing a little bit of Nina here, am I?

MARTIN. It's not about Nina or any of that –

RACHEL. Okay, well, I hoped you filled her in on the backstory, I hoped you told her The Mandela, which by the way is officially out of special measures – was sixth on a list of six, and I hope you filled her in on the appeals board and your rubbish sob story about Sam's overlooked special educational needs –

MARTIN. Well, I certainly told her about your attempt to slip him into that Catholic school in South Ken, and your sudden admiration for Cardinal Ratzinger –

RACHEL. Okay, and what about your wheeze about wangling a place at the Ascham that strangely enough foundered on five-grand-a-term fees –

MARTIN. Because you failed to locate a viable Huguenot ancestor – and yes, yes, I also told her about your brilliant harp wheeze –

RACHEL. Come on, Martin, your idea too, I think –

MARTIN. Oh no, our idea! Which was gonna make him so irresistible to that grammar in Fulham –

RACHEL. Well, I just happened to know they still don't have a harpist in the school orchestra –

MARTIN. – not to mention forcing him through various entrance exams, the sum total of which is we ended up with number six or nothing –

RACHEL. – whilst you, meanwhile, found refuge in the arms of a sexy young lawyer unencumbered with kids, so don't you – don't you –

Pause.

MARTIN. Rachel, be honest, remember how queasy we felt walking him round –

RACHEL. My school is a miracle, the kids that come in – sixty languages – the world beats a path to that school – and if you look at the, look at the value-added –

MARTIN. Which is always a pretty desperate measure –

RACHEL. Okay, I know what this is, I think what you fear, not Sam, what *you* fear is the kids at Mandela are all just a little bit too brown for you, Martin –

MARTIN. Oh fuck, Rach, nice one, playing that one, pulling that one on me – but, okay, just how many white middle-class kids are in there? Who's gonna be Sam's buddies, his peers? Realistically? Because you know very well he will be in an absolute minority of one. How many Sams are there?

RACHEL. Very few, as you know, precisely because they all think like you, and if we had even ten of them in any given year we could turn that school around –

MARTIN. Yeah, fine, but how many now? How many right now, Rachel! Four, right, four, in the whole school – two of whom have been bullied into submission, one of whom deals in prescription drugs on the Uxbridge Road and the other the child of evangelicals who see it as good preparation for a life in Mission. Or maybe I'm wrong. Am I wrong, Rach?

SAM *walks in with some bags, his hair over his face; he clocks them.*

SAM. Oh. Hey, Mum.

RACHEL. Hi, hi, love.

She embraces him.

What do you think? Of the colour? Don't you think this colour is excellent?

SAM. It's sort of – dark.

MARTIN *makes a pathetic little cheer.*

MARTIN. Good answer.

RACHEL. I reckon it'll grow on you.

MARTIN. You get anything good?

SAM. Yeah. I got *The Two Towers*.

MARTIN. *The Two Towers*! *The Two Towers* is the best.

RACHEL. What's, what's *The Two Towers*? That a computer game?

MARTIN. Ah, this is what we're up against, mate.

SAM. Yeah. Yeah.

MARTIN. Gaping holes in her cultural education.

RACHEL. Do you mind just telling me what the fucking *Two Towers* is.

SAM *looks shocked at her ferocity.*

SAM. Just a book. Dad said 'buy yourself a decent book'.

SAM *walks off.*

MARTIN. Tolkien. Nice one, Rach.

RACHEL. Of course. J. R. bloody Tolkien.

MARTIN. J. R. R. Tolkien.

> RACHEL, *to contain herself, goes back to painting;*
> MARTIN *to sorting the books.*

> Okay. '*Captain Corelli's Whanger.*'

> '*Life of Pi*', '*Fever Pitch*', '*White Teeth*'.

> Ah. Hang on. '*American Psycho.*'

RACHEL. Mine.

MARTIN. In what way is it yours?

RACHEL. I bought it.

MARTIN. For me. For my birthday.

RACHEL. Got the receipt somewhere.

MARTIN. This is getting petty.

RACHEL. Oh, this could get way more petty.

MARTIN. You refused to read it, you said you'd never have
bought it me if you'd known it was so violent.

RACHEL. It is. Sickeningly violent. Not to say misogynist.
Glib and misogynist.

MARTIN. Then allow me to spare you its violence and misogyny.

RACHEL. No chance. Mine. I'll flog it on eBay for ten pence,
five pence, postage paid.

MARTIN. Okay, I'll buy it back from eBay.

RACHEL. Okay then, I'll give to Mind. Given it's a product of
a sick mind.

MARTIN. Will you never – ever – accept that the representation
of misogyny is not in itself misogynistic?

RACHEL. Never. I'm old-fashioned that way.

> *He brings her the book; she doesn't accept it. He looks at the*
> *door she's painting.*

MARTIN. Primed and painted that in 1990.

Spent the summer doing this place up, remember what a wreck it was?

Moved from that slum on the Goldhawk Road. I'd just got off the dole, we called it 'the dole' – dole, housing benefit. Great time to be poor. That nice old lady Mrs Thatcher. You'd started teaching, but really you were about to get a gig with the LSO, and I'd finish my PhD on public housing – least we bought property before it went stellar –

RACHEL. – then everyone started moving out to Devon or Warwickshire, how we tut-tutted, 'cos we had Sam by then, and it was working with Sam, bringing Sam up here. Ethically! In the community. 'Multiculturally.'

MARTIN. That was then.

RACHEL. Yeah. Good times.

Suddenly she kisses him.

Does she do that? Does she hold your face like that? Would it have made any difference if I'd married you?

MARTIN. Rach, please.

RACHEL. Look at me. Having intended to be dignified.

I bet she's taut. I bet her pelvic floor's tight as a snare drum.

MARTIN *moves away.*

MARTIN. At that budget meeting. I resigned.

RACHEL. You resigned?

MARTIN. Posted my resignation letter on the council website under the 'News' section. Pretty good letter. I drew attention to the council motto: '*Pro Civibus et Civitate*' – 'For citizens and state', stressing the indelible link between the two, the indelible link – I said if we keep up what we're doing, driving council tax down, begrudging the few common resources we can afford, in five years' time there won't be a park that's not turned over to some property developer, legal aid forget it, all spec lawyers and pro bono, housing all be raffled off and the poor exported to some shithole in Uxbridge, there'll be a tent city of wheelchair-bound people sleeping out on Shepherd's Bush Green.

RACHEL. You stuck all that on the council website?

MARTIN. Yeah.

RACHEL. Wow. Good for you, Martin. Is it still there?

MARTIN. No. The adjudicator removed it ten minutes later. Fortunately I got my resignation e-mail in before the sacking one arrived.

RACHEL. Why are you doing all this?

MARTIN. Because I'm forty-five and I'm getting out!

RACHEL. 'Out'?

Pause.

MARTIN. Out of London.

RACHEL. What?

MARTIN. Nina has this… job. In Bicester. I think it's Bicester.

RACHEL. What is this? Bicester?

MARTIN. Yup. Well, just outside –

RACHEL. Bicester? Do you even know where Bicester is?

MARTIN. Don't be ridiculous, of course –

RACHEL. What about Sam?

MARTIN. This is the thing. This is what I wanted to talk to you about.

RACHEL. Hang on, hang on.

MARTIN. There's a really good school there, a grammar, excellent by all accounts, just out of town. And I thought, and Nina agreed, maybe we could take him down there, this weekend, and I recognise this is moving very fast, but just –

RACHEL. No. No way. You are not, that woman's not kidnapping –

MARTIN. Oh, for God's sake –

RACHEL. He can't go, he won't want to go.

MARTIN. No, he seemed really keen, which surprised me.

RACHEL. You've, you mean you've already suggested it.

MARTIN. Of course. Over lunch. Of course.

RACHEL. You – ? Sam?

MARTIN. Don't bring him into this, that's not –

RACHEL. Sam!

MARTIN. I am endeavouring to sort out a permanent solution to his educational needs, Nina is right behind it –

RACHEL. She's so fucking greedy, steals you, now my son from me as well.

MARTIN. I thought maybe, maybe you could relocate too.

RACHEL. Oh, thanks a lot, a new life in lovely Bicester.

MARTIN. The world doesn't stop at the M25. Darkness does not descend at Ealing. When did you get to be so parochial?

RACHEL. 'Parochial'? Sam's growing up in a World City. He is not going to fester in a cathedral town.

MARTIN. Bicester doesn't actually have a cathedral.

The thing is the school is… a grammar, well, a former grammar.

But Nina says there's a scholarship she could probably wing. Sam wouldn't have to board or anything. It's not my style, but –

RACHEL. No, Martin, no, what you should do is go to Nina, take her to Bicester, knock her up and get your own Little Lord Fauntleroy – Sam is a Londoner.

MARTIN. Fine. Fine. I said you'd be reasonable, she said – fine, we'll check the legal position and –

RACHEL. Legal position?

MARTIN. It's in the Cotswolds, well, edge of. You know what, it's not a crime to want to live in the Cotswolds.

Silence. RACHEL *doesn't know what to say.*

Do you want my key?

She looks at him. He offers her the key. She goes back to the painting.

SAM *comes in with his bag. A moment.*

RACHEL. Leave us alone. For a bit.

MARTIN. Well. The thing is, I'm on a meter.

RACHEL. Pay the fu – the fine then.

MARTIN. Okay. You won't try and change his –

RACHEL. Can you just get out of my house, please?

MARTIN *goes.*

So, Sam, so you talked to your dad, right?

SAM. Yeah.

RACHEL. And you've packed some stuff.

SAM. Yeah.

She looks in his bag.

RACHEL. Right. So. That's okay. Have you got enough pants for the week?

SAM. Less than a week.

I'll be back Thursday.

RACHEL. Yeah. You will. I'll have painted your room by then.

SAM. You said I could paint my room.

RACHEL. Oh. So I did. So I did.

Blackout.

Scene Two

The next day. NICK *and* LARA*'s house. Similiar to* RACHEL*'s, in fact almost identical.* NICK *is standing speaking, wandering about;* PARVEZ (PAV) *sits with his laptop, tapping away;* LARA *sits tapping into her iPhone. Glasses of red wine.* RACHEL *stands in the doorway, light of a summer evening behind her.*

NICK. So I ask very politely –

LARA. Ha! I can so imagine that.

NICK. I asked with extreme politeness, truly an old-world courtesy now vanished from the earth –

PAV. Okay, Lara, pinging the spec out to you all –

NICK. Okay, an entirely bogus patina of warmth and charm, so I say, 'Okay, so yes, I am here as a representative of SBFSI' to which she looks frankly baffled –

LARA. Now come on, where's our brand recognition – we need a proper name!

NICK. Try the acronym first, then spell it out, I say, 'You know SBFSI, obviously not the most euphonious of abbreviations – Shepherd's Bush Free School Initiative.'

LARA. Nick, don't begin by being an arsehole –

NICK. I do think we need a name – something Latinate?

PAV. I still think The Bush Academy is good.

LARA. Oh yeah, imagine it – 'You going up The Bush'?

PAV *and* LARA *laugh.*

NICK. Actually, I was very far from being an arsehole, and listen, listen, this is the Access Officer, dripping with MAs, she comes back in this lumpen way with, 'Sorry, I don't know what "euphonious" means.'

LARA. I think we can assume she was winding you up, love – this it, Pav?

West12 Shopping Centre. Hardly Harrow.

PAV. Yeah, well, beggars and choosers.

NICK. I said, 'I am sorry you don't understand the meaning of "euphonious" which is a word I have always been enormously fond of,' and, then, immediately she gives the tart rejoinder, 'I didn't go to public school,' so I said, 'It hardly takes public school to teach you the meaning of "euphonious", there have been, since the days of Dr Johnson, these rather large books stuffed to the gills with *words* that can be found in public libraries entirely free of charge and indeed are now online – '

LARA. Cut to the chase, love. Yes.

PAV. One thousand two hundred square foot floorspace. Next to Morrisons.

LARA. Minimum is fifty thousand for two-form entry.

PAV. Basically, there's a car park out back, section of which that could be converted to a play area. Rip up the tarmac and when extra units become available…

LARA. Nick, look.

NICK. Anyway, I didn't, in short, get the requisite data.

PAV. Yeah, we kinda need that stuff for the DfE meeting.

LARA. Ah. Okay. Which we now have a date for.

PAV. Wicked, Lar.

LARA. Yeah, this week. After all this time, suddenly it has to be this week.

PAV. This place is speculative, we've not got any prospective Heads.

NICK. Okay, this week, great, fine, bring it on.

RACHEL. Sorry. Hello. Hello. Sorry, I was trying to –

NICK. What?

RACHEL. Just, the door was ajar, the bell was broken, I knocked but – hello.

They all turn to look at RACHEL.

– I just came in – and I didn't want to interrupt.

LARA. No, it's fine, come in, come in. Hey, come in, properly. I'm Lara. Lara Orme.

PAV. Caught us in full flow. Him in full flow.

NICK. Not the most auspicious of introductions.

RACHEL. You're… Nick. I think I e-mailed you – Nick?

NICK. Me?

RACHEL. You are Nick, I'm pretty sure I e-mailed –

LARA. No guarantee of anything.

RACHEL. Rachel? Rachel De Witt?

NICK. My inbox is like a crime scene.

PAV. Okay, Rachel, got her here, yeah, it gets fed to my –

RACHEL. Well. That's okay then. Sorry, you're – ?

LARA. You must think we're a right shower.

PAV. Yeah, I'm Pav, okay?

NICK. Rachel De what?

RACHEL. De Witt.

PAV. De Witt?

NICK. Is that Dutch?

RACHEL. Oh. Originally Huguenot, way back, I'm told, but –

NICK. Okay, okay, yes you'd picked up our flyer, you were intrigued but unsure, would it be all right to… et cetera, et cetera. De Witt!

RACHEL. That's right, that's me.

LARA. Flyer-drop's paying off.

PAV. Nobody from the White City estate. I'm guessing you're – not –

LARA. Welcome. To. This.

RACHEL. Thanks. But, is this it? I mean, are you – it?

LARA. Us? This? No.

PAV. What this, no – there's –

LARA. How many? I mean, on –

PAV. The steering committee – how many?

NICK. Ten of us – right, red, lager or white?

RACHEL. Of what? Oh? White?

LARA. Yes, but signed up –

PAV. Oh, double figures, easily. Easily.

RACHEL. You sound quite defensive. If you don't mind me saying.

RACHEL *laughs nervously.*

LARA. Do we? Well. There's a lot at stake.

NICK. You've seen the flak we get? I mean, for God's sake, we wanna open a school in Shepherd's Bush, not a madrasa in Golders Green.

LARA. Nick. She might think you're –

PAV. He is. Isn't he? 'Strong opinions from the outset.'

NICK. Oh, come on, love, Pav's hardly going to take umbrage at –

Pav, you didn't take any umbrage from –

PAV. Might want to rein it in. A touch. Mate.

LARA. Not least because if I were Rachel here I might just find this a tiny bit off-putting.

RACHEL. No. No. Bracing stuff. But, I'll be honest with you, I don't know where I stand. Or maybe in fact I do, and this is, probably – a mistake.

NICK. Don't go. On account of my robust banter.

You need to know who we are and what we want, before you leave this room, counter all that disinformation out there. So, okay. Let's do our thing, people.

LARA. Oh. Nick. No. We don't need to. It's all on the site. Please.

NICK. No, no, come on, this is what we do, our conch moment, our 'bang the Black Rod' thing –

PAV. You bang your own rod, mate.

NICK. Ha! Good one, Pav.

RACHEL. What's this?

LARA. Just a, just a – ritual?

PAV. Something we did when we started out –

NICK. To show we are not a cabal, not just a – cabal.

LARA. Oh, fine, I'll go first, get it over with, okay, I'm Lara. Mother of Miranda, twelve, Patrick, ten, Hepzibah, eight.

NICK. We're creating our own demographic surge in West London.

LARA. Don't interrupt! Went to a bog-standard bog-standard myself. In Leicester. Learned rock-all, grafted because I do that, pretty much taught myself, got into Cambridge to my teachers' disgust, confirming their thesis that I was a pushy little cow, read Law, went into corporates, still there – and our three were in state schools, we gave it a go –

NICK. Much against my advice.

LARA. But we gave it a go, and they were unhappy, deeply –

NICK. Unschooled in the humourless idiom of 'citizenship' –

LARA. Nick, am I doing this or you? Okay, we've been doing Steiner, which is fine except it's a bit iron-your-own-muesli –

NICK. Wading through the complete works of George Steiner –

LARA. It's Rudolf Steiner, you tit – Okay, a bit precious – and we did consider, and we may still consider private –

NICK. Sadly, I earn no money and your parents are common and mine refuse to die –

LARA. Nick, they would advance you the – but that's not it, I don't think we should have to, and actually I don't like the people – I'm sorry, Nick, they are largely snobs or they're bling or – so, we thought, let's take them at their word, the Coalition, if you don't like it, do something better – I have spoken way too much.

NICK. Spoken very appositely.

LARA. So bloody patronising.

NICK. Pav.

PAV. Oh, man. Can I e-mail it you? Send you an App or something?

NICK. Pav, your spiel!

PAV. Okay, I'm in web-based design – y'know, HTML, CSS, CMS –

NICK. No one has the slightest idea what you're on about –

PAV. Got three nippers, Saff the eldest, Year Six – so – uh-oh! – and I er went to our not-so-favourite school –

RACHEL. Which one?

PAV. Oof – we don't tend to name it.

NICK. Rather like Voldemort.

RACHEL. The Mandela?

PAV. Yeah, back in the day it was the Atlee High, and already a stinker. All I recall from five years at that joint, apart from getting kicked up the ass every break by this white kid from Acton, all that remains is my last day, very last day, walking out of there, free, and being sick, literally sick with the freedom, all over my blazer. When Saff got her place with that school, no word of a lie, I said I'd torch it, 'cos there's something in the bones of that place, in the bricks.

RACHEL. But you're – you're not going to have this new school – in place for term –

PAV. I tell you, seriously, I'll go on strike if we have to. Seriously. Withhold our kids, teach them ourselves.

LARA. We can hardly do any worse.

NICK. You see what we try and do here, Rachel, is be honest. Because there's so much cant, so many euphemisms, we lie to ourselves more deeply about this issue than any other. Okay – I'm Nick Orme, unemployable, unteachable, ran some half-arsed businesses that went tits-up, oh, you know, an ill-conceived gallery of figurative painting, a back-of-the-fag-packet endeavour to plant a vineyard in Herefordshire, what did the wine taste like, Lara –

LARA. Er. Paint stripper?

NICK. And, now, here I am, verging on fifty, nothing permanent to my name – apart from my wonderful wife and wonderful family – and, oh, I should mention I am an elitist, in the strict sense of favouring elites of talent not social elites, i.e. I dig Matthew Arnold, I dig the notion that culture 'is the best that has e'er been thought and spoken', i.e. emphatically not, not, what, not – Hannah Montana. And her ilk.

LARA. You have no idea who Hannah Montana is.

NICK. Nor do I wish to.

Pause.

LARA. So – do we pass muster?

RACHEL. Oh. You, you're clearly an impressive bunch.

LARA. Oh, we are so not.

NICK. Well, I think that was sort of intended as a criticism, wasn't it?

RACHEL. I just think you come across – well, exactly as I imagined you would and why not, that's fine, thoroughly middle class, fine.

NICK. Ah – the class that dare not say its name.

RACHEL. Oh, it says it all the time, doesn't it.

And in the end I don't see how what you're doing –

LARA. Do you actually know what we're doing? Yet?

RACHEL. Well, I read your flyer. A new free school in Shepherd's Bush. Parent-run. Open to all. A fresh start.

Open to all? Really? I mean, The Mandela's open to all too, one thousand two hundred kids there, some really sharp actually. You seek the highest of standards of behaviour and learning – show me the school that doesn't, they certainly do. Some really good facilities. Tireless staff, although they are tired.

NICK. Okay. And what did you say you did? Rachel?

RACHEL. Oh, I didn't say. But as you ask, I teach at The Mandela.

Silence. RACHEL *laughs*.

Oh my God – the look on your faces.

NICK. So they're employing *agent provocateurs* now?

LARA. You might have said that. Earlier.

PAV. When did you start? Teaching?

RACHEL. Oh, aeons ago.

PAV. Okay.

RACHEL. Actually, the person you were pouring so much scorn on was my friend Jo, who certainly knows the meaning of 'euphonious' and who's been under a lot of pressure.

LARA. 'Pressure'? Give me a break. Office hours nine to five.

PAV. You here to suss us out then?

NICK. Maybe we should ask in the Cameroonian mode what could you do for us?

RACHEL. Okay, look, I really should go.

NICK. No, Rachel, I think you came here for a personal reason.

LARA. Just let her go, Nick. We've got things to do.

NICK. I think you're craving a reason to cross the floor. To enter the enemy camp, blamelessly.

PAV. Can hardly say that school's working – thirty per cent A to C GCSE, how shit is that? I'm sure you're doing your best but, babe, it's not happening.

RACHEL. Look, just admit that at the bottom of all this, there's this perception you have that your lovely children are better, do things better, deserve better and where does this perception come from, well, I guess you're the people who cut in ahead of the traffic, you're the people who jump queues, you're the early adopters, you're the first online, you know the person you need to speak to to get exactly what you want, I mean exactly – and this time you got second best and that is simply intolerable to you.

Suddenly she bursts into tears.

I'm sorry – I – I am – this is – God.

LARA. No. Hey, hey, it's – okay.

RACHEL. Now I'm really going, I shouldn't have –

LARA. Look, let me get you a cup of tea – at least.

RACHEL. I don't need a cup of tea, I didn't come here for self-help or –

LARA. You're just worried. Right? You've got kids too?

RACHEL. Yes. Yes, I do. Sam, my, yes – also eleven going on twelve and…

LARA. Sam. Sam De Witt. Of course.

NICK. Yes. Sam De Witt. He was at Brook Green?

RACHEL. What? Yes. Yes, he was.

LARA. You know I knew I recognised you. Nick, we used to see her. With her son. Cycling down the middle of Shepherd's Bush Road with the traffic backed up behind them.

RACHEL. Well, I hope we didn't inconvenience you.

Pause.

You must think I am really rude. I don't generally go into the houses of strangers and – sound off.

NICK. Why not? I do it all the time.

PAV. He really does, he really bloody does.

LARA. Look, I will get you that tea. Herbal, okay?

RACHEL. No, no, let me crawl off now and –

LARA. No. I insist. I know what this appears to be, I do, we all do.

But at the end of the day, we're neighbours, right?

LARA *goes out.*

PAV. Nick, I'll clear tomorrow, we've got the steering group at eight, report to them. You'll have another crack at getting the data-sets from the LA?

NICK. I'll go nuclear and land a Freedom of Information on them. When's the latest you need it by?

PAV. Oh. If we go on Thursday, say, Tuesday.

NICK. Ballistic missile up their jaxies.

RACHEL. Yeah, they could take up to twenty days.

NICK. I'm sorry?

RACHEL. If you do a FOI they have up to twenty days to respond.

NICK. You're kidding? But we need to know borough birth rates, school sizes, demography.

RACHEL. I'm just saying.

PAV. Okay. Shit. Well, okay, we'll just have to guesstimate it and –

NICK. So some mandarin can sit back on his pampered ass and laugh at us. What we need is a kindly mole in the public sector.

He looks at RACHEL.

RACHEL. Oh, now don't look at me.

NICK. May a man not look where he wishes in his own home?

PAV. No pressure. Great. Okay. Homewards. I'll see you tomorrow night. Defectors or Nettle?

NICK. Oh, The Nettle I think.

PAV. Safe. Goodnight, Miss De Witt.

RACHEL. Oh. Rachel. Yeah. Apologies for my – I sense, you know, I see your intentions are –

PAV. Used to think being a parent was like what you did at the weekends. But you can't leave anything to anyone else these days. Especially teachers. Joke.

PAV goes. NICK and RACHEL stand around.

RACHEL. God, is that scarab? On the walls?

NICK. Yeah. Lara thinks it's too dark. I like it. Womb-like.

RACHEL. I like it too.

LARA comes in with a cup of tea.

LARA. We only had fennel.

RACHEL. Fennel's fine.

Blackout.

Scene Three

The following evening. NICK and RACHEL on the roof garden of a Shepherd's Bush pub, drinking wine. It's hot and dark and periodically sirens rip through the night.

NICK. There's usually more of us. They all swan off to Istria when you need them.

RACHEL. Don't feel I've entirely clicked with some of them.

NICK. Yeah, he solves a lot of problems for us... Pav. But, yes, he's a bit of a mystery. I imagine he's Muslim but it never crops up, which is a relief because... Lara says his little girl wears one of those, one of the more discreet – thingies.

RACHEL. Hijabs.

NICK. Thank you – constantly get them mixed up – niqabs, hijabs, burkas. Incidentally, we'll have none of that, right. I'm with Sarkozy on this one! No yarmulkes, crucifixes and no – what's the official line on Sikhs?

RACHEL. Look, I'd better go.

NICK. No, you have to kill off this little minx of a wine with me.

RACHEL. No, Nick, really – I have to –

NICK. What have you got to get back to?

Is it that son of yours? Bring him over, I'll stand him a shandy or something.

RACHEL. No, he's with – he's with my... ex.

NICK. I do envy you on that. I was on parent duty today, and they were driving me gaga, as is their human right, so I said, 'Okay, everyone, consoles off, Crocs on, we are going for a walk,' frogmarched the little buggers out the house, dragging their feet, fighting the sheer swim of humanity, wincing at every broken-looking being, every tangled-eyed wino, every teen-mum hacking her buggy along – I mean, did you see any – any actual poverty in your childhood?

RACHEL. No, actually, I don't think I did – not like that –

NICK. So we blunder on down to Hammersmith Bridge – just to look at the Thames, to look at something not human, something grand – but I saw it through their eyes, I thought what a disgusting river you are, what a greasy, swollen, turbid thing you are, even the birds that thrive in you are dirty, mangy-looking cormorants who look like they feast on shit all day long, not even a current of cool air coming off the water – and I thought, God. I mean, why do we live here, y'know?

RACHEL. You don't really like people very much, do you, Nick?

NICK. Not in the abstract, no. Why I could never teach – end of the day, you can't sack them, can you, the kids?

RACHEL. No. Sadly. I find it very hard to hate them, even when they're openly offensive, calling you 'Miss' with not a scintilla of respect, might as well say 'Oi, slag'.

NICK*'s pouring out more wine.*

Whoa, that is enough of that –

NICK. I would find that very hard.

RACHEL. But, still, they're rather magnificent. The way they size it down. They say 'this is my life', the life you, sorry, you maunder about, well, they know no other.

NICK. I sense you still think badly of us, of... me.

RACHEL. Nick, what I think is, if you want change, change the system from within. Be a governor. Run a club. Be on the PTA. Y'know.

NICK. Ah, but what if the system's broken. Broken from the off –

RACHEL. How is it broken? Millions of kids pass through our schools, perfectly happy, enlarged, educated –

NICK. I think there was a real chance in 1944, a real chance to get it right – if they'd bought up the private schools, say, if they'd bought out the churches, if they'd truly started from scratch, then maybe – but they funked it – a few decent grammars but no, couldn't be permitted, little havens of quality, no, let's get rid of that too, bring on the comprehensive – I ask you, Rachel, what is a comprehensive but a machine for dumbing-down – they blew up the tower blocks but they didn't have the balls to dynamite the comprehensives –

RACHEL. What do you actually know about comprehensives anyway?

NICK. First-hand experience.

RACHEL. Oh, come on. How? I bet you've never been inside one.

NICK. How much? How much would you wager?

RACHEL. Fiver.

NICK. Done. I went to Holland Park. I am a survivor of Holland Park. So, yes. Cough up.

RACHEL. I need evidence.

NICK. I bear the scars. Despite the mellifluous tones I am an utter fraud. Dad whipped me out when he realised I was shaping up to be a complete weed-dazed slacker of the first order. Sent me to St Paul's, who sorted me out, double-quick. Five pounds.

She hands it over; he waves it away.

RACHEL. Right – so it didn't work for you, okay – but, Nick, it has to be better than writing off two thirds of kids to – secondary moderns – consigning them to failure from eleven –

NICK. But that's it, there's your mistake, the misconception –

RACHEL. What?

NICK. We confuse fairness with education, we muddle up equal opps with something that's by its nature about failure or success – this is what we have done as a nation, kidding ourselves education is for everyone on everyone's terms – but, Rachel, isn't education meant to be difficult – and if it's not difficult surely it makes no sense whatsoever – ?

RACHEL. If your plans prevail, you will rake off money from ordinary schools – right – rob money and kids, right – so how's that going to help solve your – conundrum?

NICK. Then they will have to raise their game, will they not? Throw down the gauntlet – besides, there's more kids than places, the state's losing them, to independent schools, half of the kids around here are leached to private schools, eye-watering fees – leaving schools like The Mandela as monopoly providers – in business, that's –

RACHEL. No, hang on, not true, no, it's not, it's in competition with all the other schools –

NICK. It's a monopoly provider if you're not smart enough to have property the right side of the park, or you aren't prepared to go to Rome, or dissemble Anglicanism, or you don't have ten k knocking about – now, you do accept that – well, you can hardly deny it. Who makes the cut in the end –

do you? No, the LA and the school and the housing market –
you get what you're given and – that's your Sam's whole life
laid out, right, am I right – because you got school number
six! And I'm sorry, I honestly don't want my kids to be me,
rising fifty, zero pension – they're gonna need their ten A
stars, their ten A-starred stars, their four A-starred A levels,
their first-class degree, their Russell Group MA – every
second of every hour on it, education, education, one false
move – one false move – and what are you? You're nothing.
I'm sorry, I'm hectoring you.

Pause.

RACHEL. Okay. Been in teaching for twenty years. If it's
broken I probably played a part.

NICK. Don't be silly, I don't blame individuals.

RACHEL. And I went in like you, all for change, it was gonna
be change through music, yes, I was an evangelist for music.
Tried to set up a scratch orchestra in my probation year, all
of twenty-two: the NUT Rep said I was elitist, racist even –
okay, there was a steel-pan band and a gospel choir, both of
which were great, but I just thought a school should have an
orchestra – anyway, I called a meeting, twenty or so kids
showed, mainly girls, okay – and I think two of them had
instruments, oddly enough a French horn and a – fiddle. So I
went to every orchestra in town, every player I knew and I
begged and borrowed and – and at the end of that year, we
put together a scratch performance of something, what was
it, oh my God, yes, Holst, 'Mars, the Bringer of War' –
Holst –

NICK *does the portentous chords of 'Mars'; RACHEL joins
in.*

Stop it, oh, you had to hear it, Nick, it was so fucking
terrible! Pure – cacophony.

NICK *does it again.*

Okay, but it was a beginning.

NICK. Good for you. They should have made you head teacher.

RACHEL. The Head didn't come. Well, wasn't popular. Some colleagues claimed it was a distraction, in an exam term, oh, I'd pulled people out of lessons, to what end, for a fairly rubbishy – I think five parents came to see it, five – and worst of all, saw these kids in the front row laughing at it, audibly, nobody rebuking them, as if there was a general consensus that I'd overreached myself, that the kids in my orchestra, that I'd somehow, I dunno, made fools of them. Martin, my, my ex said it, perhaps I'd imposed middle-class values on –

NICK. He said that?

RACHEL. Oh, he was probably right.

NICK. Was Mozart middle class? Child prodigy, debtors ever at the door – was Beethoven middle class? Deaf as a post, broke – or Mahler, what was he, a Jew, son of an innkeeper?

RACHEL. Well, it was all music-tech and ditties from thereon in – but I still – when Sam started fiddle, I opened up the workbook for Grade One music, opened it up, and there it was, just as it always has been – time signatures, note values, dynamics – just the same, just what I had to learn, just as hard, just as clear. I mean, call me a reactionary but I do find that, I dunno, comforting...

NICK. Is it reactionary to teach algebra? Is it reactionary to learn to draw perspective? Is it reactionary to learn to write in copperplate?

RACHEL. Maybe it is. Maybe people like you and me are redundant. I'm not sure the world needs us, needs any more arts graduates with humanist values. Sorry – not actually thought about all that... didn't get much sleep last night. Painting in the small hours –

NICK. You should always paint in natural light.

Pause.

When did he – go? I take it he did. Go. Your odious ex.

RACHEL. What? No, sorry. No. Can we not get in to this?

NICK. But... sorry. Just I sense this is all recent. Raw.

RACHEL. Nick, as I say, will you stay off this, please.

NICK. Okay. Okay. Sure.

He touches her.

But if at another time...

RACHEL. Hey! I didn't come here tonight 'cos I am on the rebound, okay.

NICK. Just a disinterested gesture.

RACHEL. Well, thanks, thank you for your disinterest!

They both laugh at this.

NICK. What did he do? Your ex?

RACHEL. Martin. He worked for the LA.

NICK. Interesting. What does he – what area did he work in?

RACHEL. Housing. Why are we talking about him?

NICK. Very interesting. I mean, presumably you know how to get into his e-mail account?

RACHEL. I know his password, his log-in, he always uses his date of birth, he's pretty unimaginative... Martin.

NICK. How about having a rummage around, see if you can find anything of interest to us? Anything of a demographic nature?

Pause. RACHEL *looks at* NICK.

RACHEL. I will now say goodnight before I get in to any more –

NICK. Resign and work for us.

RACHEL. I'm sorry?

NICK. Resign and work for us.

RACHEL. Oh. Resign and work for – you –

She laughs.

NICK. Yeah. It, us.

RACHEL. Even though 'it', 'us' does not exist.

NICK. Look, you've done your time in the mission station, Rachel. You've served your sentence in the salt mines. Be our head teacher.

RACHEL. Oh, that's utterly ridiculous, as you know. You need some training and – years of –

NICK. Why is it? Who says so? Everything's up for grabs.

This is a free school, right, we set the terms –

RACHEL. I have absolutely no management experience. I mean, okay, I used to run a department, but –

NICK. There you are! And you'd have all of us behind you. You'd be wonderful.

RACHEL. And the only thing I know about with any confidence is music.

NICK. Exactly! And we will put music at the heart of everything we do. We will make musical aptitude a key element in admissions –

RACHEL. Nick, you can't, that would be – divisive –

NICK. They will play Holst to study astronomy, they will play Beethoven to study the Enlightenment, Bach as the way into maths, Mozart's libretti as the way into languages, every day a recital, every term a concert, forget about SATs and keystage this and that, if they can sing it, if they can play it, they will be front-foot, outward-looking kids. I tell you, Rachel, our school will be heard before it is seen.

Sudden rush of a glorious recording of Bach's 'Double Violin Concerto'.

Scene Four

Mid-morning, Thursday. RACHEL *with* SAM*; bags.* SAM *on* RACHEL*'s laptop;* RACHEL *in painting shirt.* MARTIN *comes in with another bag.*

RACHEL. So how did you find Bicester?

MARTIN. On the M40. Left after Oxford. Ho ho.

RACHEL. How was it, Sam?

SAM. Okay. Bit weird, bit old, weird smells.

MARTIN. Good weird, though.

SAM. Weird weird.

RACHEL. Oh, and tell me about the lively local market.

MARTIN. That's not helpful.

RACHEL. The lovely lively local market all with stalls with brightly striped canvas roofs and not one of them selling *hijabs* or international phonecards.

MARTIN. Yes, yes, there was a market.

RACHEL. Oh, and what about the small, cosy shops run by fathers and sons selling real food, big glossy pork pies and pigs hanging by their trotters.

MARTIN. I take it you mean Waitrose.

RACHEL. Oh, and what about the all-round slower pace of life.

SAM. Yeah, Dad, I was thinking, why was everyone so old?

MARTIN. Sam, that's an exaggeration.

RACHEL. What it is, Sam, is old folk, they love places that look like places they knew in their youth, and of course with your dad getting on, the lure of kinder, calmer places like Bicester where people just stop you in the streets simply to say 'Good morning' –

SAM. Why are you being so freaky, Mum?

MARTIN. She's being satirical. She thinks.

RACHEL. Places a bit like the Shire –

SAM. 'The Shire'?

RACHEL. You know. Where Bilbo lives.

SAM. You getting into Tolkien, Mum? Excellent!

RACHEL. I thought I'd give *The Hobbit* a go.

MARTIN. For God's sake, Rach.

RACHEL. But seriously, most importantly of all, how was the school?

MARTIN. Sam, pop next door, will you.

RACHEL. But I bet it was so nice. Was it nice? All turrets and towers like Hogwarts. Oh, and I bet the facilities are good.

SAM. Quite cool. They have like this big new like theatre.

RACHEL. Swimming pool?

SAM. Yes.

RACHEL. Large grounds, mature trees, polished dark wood?

MARTIN. Sam, mate, take it next door, now, okay?

SAM *goes off.*

So. Here's the situation. They can fit him in next term.

RACHEL. Oh. Great. What luck.

MARTIN. Of course, term doesn't start til mid-September –

RACHEL. Well, that's public schools. Work-shy masters with scholarly hobbies. Mind you, they must be itching to get back into full-time pederasty.

MARTIN. You know this, this is… below you.

RACHEL. Oh, there is no 'below me', Martin. Believe me, I've checked. By the way, is that a stud in your ear?

MARTIN. Yes. Maybe.

RACHEL. It looks silly.

MARTIN. This is a waste of time, but you know what, he had fun this week. He was knocked out by the place, as was I, really clicked with the master – the teacher – I was surprised how – and it's actually very multicultural, tiny class sizes –

RACHEL. Martin, this week, while Sam was gone, I took it upon myself to take some steps. Which might not necessitate him going to The Mandela.

Pause.

MARTIN. Right. What steps might those be?

RACHEL. Well, step one, in the short term, withholding him from it, from the school.

MARTIN. Right. Okay. So, what, home-schooling him?

RACHEL. In the first instance, yes.

MARTIN. But what about… work?

RACHEL. Well, I'd have to resign. Take a leaf out of your book.

MARTIN. Okay – and then when you two have gone insane with boredom –

RACHEL. I said that was the first step. So, so you might want to look at this.

She hands him a document. He leafs through. Laughs.

MARTIN. Yeah, what has this got to do with you and Sam?

RACHEL. Yes, typically you object before you know anything about it.

MARTIN. What do I need to know, we know what free schools are, you of all people are well aware they're Trojan horses for –

RACHEL. Okay, where did you get that from? Polly Toynbee?

MARTIN. Possibly – would that be a problem if I read Polly Toynbee?

RACHEL. It's not what it may seem. The people involved –

MARTIN. Yeah, who are the people involved? Hedge-fund managers, loss-adjusters, property speculators?

RACHEL. There's writers, lawyers, web designers. Entrepreneurs. There's even a potter involved.

MARTIN. Any teachers? Or would that be conceding too much to professional expertise?

RACHEL. Well, yes – were I to get involved –

MARTIN. Were you to get involved? How would you get involved?

RACHEL. So now I need your permission?

MARTIN. Okay, and I see it's headed up by Mr Nick Orme. I take it you know who this guy is? Spends his entire life harassing my former colleagues.

RACHEL. Nick's just, just chairing it, the parent group, he gives generously of his time, he's charming, passionate.

MARTIN. Yeah yeah and presumably his school's teachings will be in accordance with the National Curriculum –

RACHEL. You've spent your whole life slagging off the National Curriculum.

MARTIN. I prefer it to the Gospel according to Nick Orme.

RACHEL. The entire point of being a free school is to break loose from the shackles of the state.

MARTIN. 'The shackles of the state'? My God. You're a state schoolteacher, aren't you?

RACHEL. And how has that served me, how is that serving Sam? Whatever the state is, and I don't pretend to know any more, round here it doesn't work. Look at you, Martin, look what you're doing too.

MARTIN. What has happened this week? Did the Coalition come calling by any chance?

RACHEL. I don't need any lectures from you, Mr White Flight.

Pause.

MARTIN. Look, Rachel, okay, in all seriousness – who are these people?

I mean, what are their credentials? These people you seem intent on abandoning our son to – what are they – have they, say, been CRB'd? And what half-baked crap will they be teaching, because we know this whole thing is handing the keys to every malcontent fruitcake –

RACHEL. Ah, such clichéd – crap –

MARTIN. But, okay, will they be Ofstedded? Are their premises licensed, are they kosher on health and safety – I am serious – who are these cranks?

RACHEL. 'These cranks', Martin, are our community, well, my community.

MARTIN. Oh, okay, right, of course, the Big Society, yes! The Little Platoons!

RACHEL. Maybe, maybe – and I may not agree with them all, and I may not like them, and I might just find myself at odds with them every step of the way, but they are my neighbours, and they want to make a difference here, in this place, where we live and I can get behind that even if you can't.

Pause.

MARTIN. Okay. This is my fault, okay, I am sorry this has all been very difficult for you, I see that. But, Rach, how can I let you do this?

RACHEL. How will you stop me? Look, if I can get something going here that's good, that's real education, then that's got to be the best solution – for Sam, for you and, okay, maybe for – her.

MARTIN. Look, we're both under tremendous pressure, I grant you that –

RACHEL. Martin, you are not going to change my mind so don't –

MARTIN. Rachel you are aligning yourself with a bunch of pushy posh wankers setting out –

RACHEL. 'Posh'! – I like that, you getting yourself sucked off
by – some lawyer!

MARTIN. – mounting a coup against the public sector – who –

RACHEL. 'A coup'! This is, this is the public fucking sector –
and –

MARTIN. Have you told your colleagues? Is Jo cool with it?
What about everyone at The Mandela? You think they're
gonna take this lying down?

RACHEL. The moment you walked out that door you lost the
right to say any damn thing about what I do with my life,
Martin!

SAM *comes in.*

SAM. I am trying to read my bloody fucking book!

They look at him, horrified.

RACHEL. Sam. Sorry. It's okay.

SAM *throws his book down and walks off.*

Sam!

MARTIN. It won't work. It can't work. You know that. This
community doesn't want this. This community won't allow
this to happen. And you might save some hurt – if we
acknowledged that now.

RACHEL. Oh, it's going to work, Martin. It has to.

MARTIN. You're thrashing about, trying to find a solution,
you're –

RACHEL. Actually, I feel like I've woken up. After a long,
confused sleep. I feel like suddenly I am alive and active and
full of purpose.

MARTIN. Well, I hope the feeling lasts.

Blackout.

Scene Five

Mid-morning, Thursday. A functional room in the Department of Education. LARA, PAV, dressed to kill. They wait. LARA is frantically texting. There's a picture of Michael Gove in a school on the wall.

LARA. He did this on our first date, he did this at our wedding, he was even late when my waters broke.

PAV. He's a genuine chancer is Nick.

LARA. We all have to share his enthusiasms – last year, it was the allotment. Oh, we were going to grow everything, going to be self-sufficient, we were out there rotivating it, double-digging it, planting it out, oh, and Nick read everything, yes, six-month crash course in horticulture, I only just talked him out of taking on three derelict plots and declaring himself a smallholder. Then, one day, all of a sudden it was down to me, just me and Miranda, battling to grow a few mangy carrots and artichokes and drummed off by the allotment committee for neglect of tenure.

During this, PAV has got up; suddenly he whips out his phone and takes a picture of himself in front of the shot of Gove.

LARA. What are you doing?

PAV. For the family. Parvez Akhtar in a High Office of State!

You want one?

LARA. Don't be silly – no, Pav – this is embarrassing.

PAV. Smile, Lara. You look good when you smile. Should smile more often. There.

Takes a shot.

LARA. Thanks. Very nice. Do I not smile? I think I forget to.

PAV. You should never do that.

LARA. Oh, why's his bloody phone off?

PAV. Yeah, they're running late anyway, useless –

LARA. You know Nick thinks she should come.

PAV. Right. Don't see her.

LARA. I did remind him I thought we weren't going to be captured by the professionals. I find her, I don't know, shrill. That light in her eyes.

PAV. Never been the biggest fan of teachers – plus she didn't remember me. No reason she should.

LARA. I don't tend to trust evangelists. They neglect the details.

PAV. I remember her. Last year at Attlee. We all thought she was well fit. Like she had a halo around her. I think we all thought she was gonna sort it all out.

LARA. She was at your school? Sorry… how is that possible, you can only be – ?

PAV. Younger than I look, Lara. Yeah, on teaching practice or something. I remember thinking, girl, they're gonna eat you alive here. And a bit of me thinking – you sort of deserve it. I'm so not up for missionaries. This school for me is not about culture and that, it's not like some finishing school – it's got to be a proper preparation for life. That's what I needed, what I didn't get, that's what my kids are gonna need. The road map, the keys to the kingdom.

NICK *comes in.*

NICK. Ah, doesn't it make you choke, that air, the dead air of a public institution? The passive-aggressive blocking of change at every workstation. Sorry, am I very late?

LARA. Where have you been, you're fronting the bloody presentation, you idiot!

NICK. Steady on, hon. Company present.

LARA. Oh, Pav knows the score, I think.

PAV. Basically we need to play today for keeps, yeah. We don't want to look whimsical.

NICK. Of course, of course. No Ms De Witt?

PAV. Do you not think she might be a bit… superfluous? Given we barely know her, mate.

NICK. Trust my instincts. I can smell talent.

LARA. She's wayward. We've got enough waywardness.

NICK. Rachel De Witt is our human dirty bomb. Here.

He gets some documents out of a cycle-sack.

Lovely, lovely numbers, which reveal we have an unanswerable case – a shortfall of two thousand places at primary level next year and worsening through to secondary, forty-five per cent of the borough in independent schools, clear and unanswerable case for a new school.

PAV *is leafing through.*

PAV. Ah, you know what, fair dos, this is actually quite awesome.

NICK. Now they have to put us on the fast-track. No argument.

LARA. Nick, you know they won't be able to blatantly support any one project.

NICK. We're first out of the gate. We're the true believers.

PAV. Not gonna look too cool for them if they don't get any free schools in the pipeline.

NICK *looking at the picture of Gove.*

NICK. There he is, smiling down on us. One day soon, Michael, every child in this country will once again know who Miss Havisham is, how to locate Belgium on a map and the historical impact of Bismarck.

LARA. Nick, please, lay off the – personal connections – and you need to be moderate, to seem, moderate –

PAV. Sorry – 'personal connections'?

POLLY *comes in, a young Civil Servant, pretty, improbably posh.*

POLLY. Hello, hello, so sorry, so, hello, are you, is this – Mr Akhtar?

PAV. Yeah – sure – well done – what, like you guessed – ?

POLLY. Yes, yes. Because, because of the name, your name. Hello, hello, then you're Lara Orme –

LARA. Yes. Hello.

POLLY. So by a process of elimination you must be Nick?

NICK. Yup. Indisputably.

PAV *and* LARA *exchange a glance.*

POLLY. You don't have to be a genius to work here but it helps.

Okay – oh gosh, did they not get you any coffees?

Actually, never mind, it's not good coffee.

NICK. Maybe you should outsource it. To Costa.

POLLY. Excellent idea, Nick, although I'd opt for Caffè Nero.

NICK. Is Michael coming in?

POLLY. Michael? I'm sorry?

NICK. The Michael.

POLLY. Oh. The Secretary of State. Actually, no, I work for the Minister for Schools, Nick Gibb, who sends greetings, I think that Michael's out on a research trip today – opening something, closing something – oh, and I'm tasked with free schools – I'm Polly, did I say, I didn't say that, Polly Tyneham, hello.

PAV. So, basically we're talking to the right person –

LARA. Just you seem so young.

POLLY. That's such a subjective thing, isn't it? Yes, yes you are, yes you really are, I am the horse's mouth. Sit, sit down, sit down. As I say, I have the free school, er, brief, and wow – we are so delighted, excited, that so many of you, and all over the country too, so many fabulous applications, and you guys are way ahead of the game, I mean, terrifically well done, really impressive, good stuff. Okay.

NICK. Great – so that's a green light? Go forth and educate?

POLLY. Oh, look at you, you're eager, of course, but you wouldn't expect me to short-circuit our process –

LARA. We were hoping today we might get a sense of that –

PAV. The process –

POLLY. Well, there are four stages and currently you are at stage one –

NICK. Yes, Michael warned me you might do this.

POLLY. I'm sorry.

LARA. Nick.

NICK. I mean you in the generic sense, of course.

POLLY. Really? Michael – Gove – spoke with you? Gosh.

NICK. Texted me. Yeah. 'Maintain the momentum. M.' That's how he signs himself. Simple, unfussy – Aberdonian to the core. Simply 'M'.

POLLY. Why would the Secretary of State question a process he himself has devised?

NICK. We know what this is about, Polly – we are your shock troops, right, humble grunts down in the dust of Helmand, taking Taliban bullets to save your arses, right.

POLLY. That's a very colourful analogy, Nick.

NICK. And we also know you can't afford too many body bags on this one.

POLLY. So, look, as I say, there is, inevitably, a process. We've had applications from many, many groups –

NICK. Yeah, but mostly ill-thought-out, amateur –

POLLY. Groups such as yours, trying to keep a middle school open perhaps, seeking more second-language provision, people very much like yourselves, and we cannot short-circuit that process that releases tax payers' money simply because a given individual may or may not have known our Minister in a previous life. Right? I mean, that's right, isn't it?

NICK *grunts*.

PAV. But, essentially, the application's on the right lines?

POLLY. With a little more detail you might well make the approved list.

NICK. So put the weaponry up front then. We need boots on the ground, we need Stinger missiles not warm words, I mean, come on, BRING IT ON, guys, you've been in here since May –

POLLY. Right, maybe I gave out the wrong signal here, but actually, you know what, Nick, I'm really not that up for being talked to like this, okay?

Pause.

LARA. Polly, sorry, I guess, we're just very serious about this. I mean, we're all busy people, this is starting to take over our lives.

POLLY. There's no doubting your commitment.

LARA. In a way, it's like we've been sent a signal, from the Government, as if we're being egged on.

PAV. Yeah, we're living and breathing this. Lot at stake, with our kids, other people's kids.

LARA. Absolutely, it's personal, very –

POLLY. That's exactly what it should be. Personal.

LARA. Right. Good. Oh, and we didn't actually say but we really so appreciate this meeting.

PAV. Oh yeah, that you found a slot at such short notice. Don't we, mate?

Appreciate it.

NICK. What? Yes. Yes, we do.

POLLY. Okay, I'm going to commit an indiscretion. In order to do so I need your complete assurance that what I say goes no further than this room?

They look at each other.

LARA. Absolutely. Nick?

NICK. Sure.

POLLY. Right. Not everyone is on-side. Not even in this… building.

NICK. Career Civil Servants?

POLLY. Right. Who are being laid off. Who feel mutinous. Who are not consulted. I am so not part of that and I am not popular for it. I'm with you guys. I like to say yes! But, given that, given the sensitivity of this, we can't afford to take risks – yet, yet nor do we have the luxury of time. The media are crawling all over this policy, it's flattering even, the weight of expectation, honestly more than the cuts, the Health reforms, this policy has become the Coalition's touchstone. But we have many many enemies, there's a very considerable appetite for a gaffe. Okay, imagine we green-light a school, I dunno, in Salford, and in the small print they hint at their passion for Sharia law and say I didn't clock it. I would be – toast. Or imagine we back some Christian group who turn out to have a total allergy to homosexuality in all its forms – imagine the headlines in the *Guardian*. 'Bad to Be Gay? – Inside Gove's Free Schools.' Right? Absolute toast! Which is why we need to be copper-bottom-sure every free school serves the policy as a whole and does not bring that policy into disrepute.

NICK. So give us some usable feedback then, given you know the competition, stress-test us, lay it on us.

LARA. Nick, give her a break. She's on our side.

POLLY. Okay, feedback, fine, well, as I said, it's all really promising, yes, I think the premises, I saw the ground plan you faxed over, look – fine – a little small perhaps. I think your business plan is – plausible – I think the timeline's ambitious, it's very, very ambitious –

NICK. We don't have the luxury of procrastin –

POLLY. Excuse me! Thank you – the main thing – my real reservation I, we, have – and doubtless this will sound ironic coming from me – concerns, well, your... profile – your relationship to your community.

PAV. Our what? Meaning what?

LARA. Nick and I have been living in Shepherd's Bush for ten years.

POLLY. Maybe you're just a tiny bit... posh. I simply mean, sociologically, how you will, how you do – seem. Which of course shouldn't matter, should it, Nick. But sadly it does... matter. It doesn't exactly help that you're based in London, metropolitan and not only London, but West London at that – I mean, were you in South London, okay. And I need hardly make the point about your racial... complexion. Okay, not exclusively white –

PAV. Pretty brown myself, last time I checked.

NICK. As a matter of fact I'm a lesbian. From Central Anatolia. Does that help?

POLLY. No, that's not funny. Even faintly. The fact of the matter is you need to be, well, rather more embedded. In your community. Have you consulted extensively, sought support from the hard-to-reach?

LARA. We've been absolutely deluged with support.

POLLY. Yes, but from whom, Lara? What's your demographic? I hardly think you could be said to represent the whole of Shepherd's Bush. Could you?

NICK. We are the squeezed middle. The people who work, who value work. The people who value education. People with no savings, with negative equity, fearing for their old age, the concerned parents. I myself earned just over the median adult wage last year, Pav, you –

PAV. No, mate, we don't need to go into that –

NICK. Well, let's say considerably less than a Civil Service stipend.

POLLY. No, I mean, this is all good, really, this is wonderful, but all I'm saying is… well, the symbolism, is not, sadly not entirely irrelevant.

PAV. So what do you want, you saying we should all relocate to Brixton – ?

POLLY. Brixton? No, not Brixton. I live in Brixton.

NICK. Okay, Stockwell maybe.

POLLY. Stockwell might have been more the thing. Oh, and if one were to do a gap-analysis, one would have to conclude that you lack – educational expertise.

PAV. We're consulting with a number of – providers –

POLLY. Yes, but at the end of the day you will need educators, at the forefront, you'll need their blessing and their expertise. These are not insuperable problems, they're certainly not intended to blunt your purpose – but if you're to be in the first round of funding – you need to resolve them. PDQ.

So, shall we leave it there – apply end of the month, first wave green-lit early autumn, business plan in for February, and if all that passes muster, you'll open next September. Don't be discouraged by any of this. You've made so many of the appropriate first steps.

POLLY*'s getting up when* RACHEL *walks in.*

RACHEL. Oh, I am so, so sorry, for some reason had it in my head you were in Pimlico. Have I missed anything?

POLLY. Sorry, I don't seem to have anyone else on my list.

NICK. This is Rachel De Witt, our new head teacher.

PAV. What are you talking about, mate?

LARA. Nick!

RACHEL. I am not – I haven't –

NICK. Worked in sink schools all her days. Knows W12 better than anyone. Knows the shoddy teaching, the toxic racial mix and the lazy practices – oh, and not only that, she is a single mother, lone parent and she's got skin in the game, putting her own damn son in the school.

Pause.

POLLY. So, are you intending to be the head teacher of this school, Rachel?

Pause.

RACHEL. If they'll have me.

Blackout.

End of Act One.

ACT TWO

Scene One

Late afternoon, Friday, winter. A room in the newly adapted shopping-centre premises of Concordia Academy – a large shapeless space near the opening onto the mall. On the walls, handprints of children in different colours. A large sign saying: 'WORK HARD. BE NICE.' Also a quote from Michel de Montaigne: 'LEARNING IS A GREAT ORNAMENT... AND A TOOL OF MARVELLOUS UTILITY.' RACHEL is at a table, on which a huge heap of application forms is piled; SAM is reading names out as RACHEL enters them into a database.

SAM. Abdi. Er. Hussein.

RACHEL. Okay. Date of birth?

SAM. Er. 7 – 4 – 1999.

RACHEL. Address?

SAM. South Africa Road.

RACHEL. Okay. Next one.

SAM. Okay. Er – Korfa, is that – can't read it – Korfa –

RACHEL. Korfa Halane?

SAM. Yeah. 3 – 2 – 99.

RACHEL. South Africa Road again by any chance?

SAM. Yeah.

RACHEL. I detect a pattern. Halane? I think I taught his brother.

Total mayhem merchant. Requested that I beat him like his father did. Asad, that was his name. Nice lad, one to one, but a terror in a class.

SAM. Is there gonna be corporal punishment? In your school?

RACHEL. Your school. Sadly, I believe it's illegal. Who's next up?

SAM. Er. Maeve Stanley.

RACHEL. No! Let me see that – what, Pennard Road, Maeve Stanley?

SAM. Mmm. Yeah.

RACHEL. Oh. That's… that's extraordinary. That's Stephanie's girl, Steph teaches PE, big union rep, and she's applied for Maeve.

SAM. Maeve's pretty weird. Had this weird hair.

RACHEL. Unbelievable.

SAM receives a text.

Oh. Is that him?

SAM. Dunno.

RACHEL. It's him, right?

SAM shrugs.

He's going to be late? He'll have a job getting you out of London tonight.

SAM. We're not leaving London.

RACHEL. Doubt that – she'll need her pound of flesh.

Why do I always imagine her with bright red lips?

Pause.

Sam, stupid question, honest answer required, is she really pretty?

SAM. Pretty old.

RACHEL. She's younger than me. What does that make me?

SAM. She wears tons of make-up.

RACHEL. Now I'm liking this better. Do you have a picture of her? And him? On your phone? Smiling, in big jumpers, or what, white towelling dressing gowns –

SAM. I'm not enjoying this conversation.

RACHEL. No. Not fair is it, on you. Sorry.

Okay, what do we have next. Oh, cheeky, this is someone applying from Southwark. Way out of catchment.

SAM *is now reading his text. Suddenly he gets up and starts to walk out.*

What's up?

SAM. Says he's gonna be a whole hour late, stupid – twat.

RACHEL. I'm sorry. I'm sure there's a –

SAM. Yeah, why tell me now? Why not tell me an hour ago?

SAM*'s putting on his big padded coat.*

RACHEL. To be fair to him, he's – actually, why should I be fair, it's outrageous.

SAM. I'm cold. I'm hungry. Stuck in here all day, it's depressing.

RACHEL. Oh! I'm sorry you've had such a depressing day, I thought it was a good day – did you object to a particular aspect of the day?

SAM. I wasn't saying, you know I –

RACHEL. I thought we had fun, given that maths is hardly my – *métier*.

SAM. Yeah, I wasn't saying anything about you.

RACHEL. Point taken. You're very… forbearing. Okay, I have a tenner on my person. Go mad in Morrisons and buy yourself something from the bakery. And I think there's still snow on the Green. Kick it about. Go breathe in some non-West12 air. Have a smoothie. Read your book. Don't wear your iPod, it attracts attention.

SAM. Okay. Whatever.

RACHEL. Just stay on radar.

She gives him the money. He puts on his iPod earplugs and goes. RACHEL *returns to the application forms. Somewhere*

off the sound of a car alarm. She gets up to look. NICK
comes in, unseen to her, with flowers, a bottle of champagne
and a big silly heart-shaped 'Congratulations' balloon in
tow.

NICK. So I've done something silly.

RACHEL. Nick! Jesus.

NICK. Just thought we ought to strike a festive note.

RACHEL. It's not in the bag – save it for later.

NICK. It'll be a formality –

RACHEL. It's very far from that. Oh, the kids can come at half
six.

NICK. Ah, the kids, great. Fully briefed?

RACHEL. No. Why would I brief them?

NICK. I just meant… they'll know why they're here.

Anything I can put these in?

RACHEL. This is not Bedales and I am not Matron.

NICK. That's quite an image you've offered me there.

I have it – a bottle of Evian – improvisation!

He rather skilfully achieves this.

– oh, look in that bag, there are glasses –

RACHEL. Glasses?

NICK. Well, those stupid screw-on plastic-fluty things – why
don't you assemble them?

RACHEL. You're opting for the full tacky effect.

She assembles them; he has the flowers sorted.

NICK. Well, I'm a tacky kind of guy; so – there, first blooms of
spring, picked hopefully by Romanian child labour in the
Vale of Evesham. And this for after she goes – to lubricate
matters. Your genuine Party Lager. And this you will have to
forgive me for.

He hands her the balloon.

From Poundland. And yes, before you ask, it cost a pound.

RACHEL. Well. I have no idea why it's for me as such.

NICK. Oh, you think she'd – Lara wouldn't object.

RACHEL. Might be wise to give it to her, not me.

NICK. We're barely on speaking terms. She keeps throwing things at me. Slippers I could live with, but I draw the line at crockery.

Do you disapprove of me?

RACHEL. Nick, we really don't want to confuse the issue here. Do we?

They look at each other; then RACHEL *goes back to her admissions.*

NICK. Yah, prone to gestures, sorry.

Ah, bejesus, look at all those. Is that the final tally?

RACHEL. Oh, yes. Eight hundred and fifty-seven.

NICK. And they said it would never catch on.

RACHEL. When we can take, at the most, a hundred.

NICK. Eight to one's a cracking ratio. I'm sure they'll largely fall short of the criteria.

RACHEL. Oh what, the criteria that they have to be eleven and live in West London?

NICK. Yes, but we can sift them on things like musicality –

RACHEL. I don't know if we can do that, Nick.

NICK. We've made it clear they had to be interested in music –

RACHEL. We didn't even ask for any details and there's musical CVs here I envy – kids with Grade Six already, harpists, trombonists, players of period instruments –

NICK. Lovely, a consort of shawms and sackbuts playing in the new term –

RACHEL. Yes, but we can't simply take those kids, can we? Look, look at all these – all these are from the White City estate, alone – which is absolutely technically who we serve – this one, Nasteho –

NICK. What's that? I mean. The provenance of – ?

RACHEL. Somali, I think, aged eleven, three brothers, 'I love the idea of your school and would love to be part of it; I sing, I freestyle, I am musical,' signed in lieu of his – no, her mother –

NICK. Probably just chancing her arm.

RACHEL. Oh, you know that, do you? There must be fifty like that at least.

NICK. Right.

RACHEL. Which is, of course, great news. I guess, I imagined... those who applied might, I don't know...

NICK. Self-select?

RACHEL. No. I don't know. But how do we even begin to deliver on this to all of these... children?

NICK. Rachel, this is the proof of the pudding, right. They said there was no demand. They said it would only be Jemimas and Jeremys. This, all this says they were wrong. We are officially oversubscribed, so the oversubscription criteria need to kick in.

RACHEL. The only criteria is distance from their door to that door. The closer you are, the clearer your right to come.

NICK. Then we use our whole three-mile radius. Presumably we can finesse it a bit.

RACHEL. How would we do that? Any direction from here, throw a three-mile net, you hit the poor. Because of course, of course that's the only fair way to do it – of course – because we are obliged to serve this community, in the end.

NICK. Tell me this, why are state schools the last place on earth where fairness applies?

RACHEL. Oh Nick, please –

NICK. But isn't that why they fail, again and again?

And did you and I choose to make Shepherd's Bush a suburb of Mogadishu?

RACHEL. Nick, that's – that's a shit thing to say. Take that back.

Pause.

NICK. Okay, okay, you know I meant nothing sinister – but, Rachel, remember this, we don't want to become just another school at the mercy of its catchment. Now, okay, as you say we have to respond to our locality – but nobody's specified how big that is – three miles, five miles, Shepherd's Bush, Hammersmith, West London, London? – A straight line from that door south, east, north, west? – You know how it works out there – only the loser schools do it strictly by the books –

RACHEL. Look, what, what are you implying? You're implying that we take from some streets and not others? That we, what, that we red-line our catchment?

NICK. We need a mechanism, Rachel. You know that. The joy and the terror of this, is that we are in the driving seat here. We actually get to play God. Admittedly a God constrained by a somewhat leaky admissions code. The governors set the terms and as long as those terms are transparent and we can stand by them, they stand. I know what concerns you, and it's an honourable concern – but you really don't want to reinvent the wheel here, do you?

LARA *comes in in a suit.*

LARA. Oh. So you are here. Of course.

NICK. Yes. And I was on time, I think.

RACHEL. Yes, we really better get started – where's Pav?

LARA. You promised you would pick up the fucking kids.

NICK. Hey, language – Kasha's on it.

RACHEL. Oh, did we say hello, Lara?

LARA. Kasha is away, you knew this was her weekend off.

RACHEL. So you'll be taking minutes?

LARA. Kasha is away and I got a call from Steiner to say they were locking up the building and our children were in tears.

NICK. And they say they offer wrap-around learning.

LARA. I had to leave my meeting, had to drive them home, stick them in front of CBBC, leaving Miranda *in loco parentis*, which as she rightly pointed out is illegal, whilst also reminding me that the Steiner ethos strictly forbids the indiscriminate use of television – Jesus, Nick, I despair –

NICK. Those hippies should take a bit more responsibility –

LARA. They're not hippies, they're not German or hippies as you tirelessly say and they have kids of their own –

RACHEL. I'm sorry to interrupt – but I don't think we should wait, I think we need to start.

LARA unloads a whole bunch of documents and pulls out a salad from Pret A Manger, which she gobbles down during the next sequence.

LARA. Sorry, late lunch. Okay, the business plan –

RACHEL. Oh. So are we formally starting – ?

NICK. Yes, yes, okay, apologies – we await Mr Akhtar's apologies, you've all read the minutes, okay, Lara, present the business plan –

LARA. Pav was meant to give it the once-over –

RACHEL. I'm calling him – he seems to be making a habit of this –

LARA. Oh, I think he's got a very difficult home life at the moment –

RACHEL. Who hasn't?

NICK. What would you know about his home life?

LARA. He confides in me.

NICK. Yeah, well, be careful, look what happened to Lauren Booth.

RACHEL. Did you e-mail me the latest draft?

LARA. Okay, okay, okay, I will do it now, sorry, I only have the one brain.

LARA *is on her laptop,* RACHEL *on her phone,* NICK *doodling disconsolately.*

There, only a couple of boxes still unfilled – page ten I think, yes, took your text on the ethos pretty much verbatim, er, what else –

RACHEL. Nothing. Okay, this is great – you have a copy in front of you, Nick?

NICK. Mmm. I can see yours fine.

LARA. On budget I used union minimums on salaries, as you suggested –

RACHEL. Largely taking grads in, so you could probably take that figure down a little –

NICK. Shouldn't we have a few more veteran hands?

RACHEL. Too expensive – we need supple young grads with a taste for long hours –

LARA. Okay – and I am right in saying we will take the current little cohort into Year Eight?

RACHEL. Well, we have to.

LARA. Nick?

NICK. Run it past Polly. Might be an issue.

LARA. Yes, I thought it might be an issue – in law.

RACHEL. What do you mean, 'an issue in law'?

It has to happen. Otherwise, otherwise what about provision for Sam – or for Miranda?

NICK *looks at* LARA *who refuses to meet his glare;* RACHEL *notices this.*

Oh and, by the way, I thought she was ill, Miranda.

LARA. Aren't we sticking to the agenda?

NICK. We should stick to the agenda. Okay, so budget is good, governance is good, exclusion policy –

LARA. This bit again needs, page four, now I wasn't sure what we'd decided: 'Details of any organisations that may be involved in delivering the school, including whether, and if so how, the proposer intends to procure a management company and/or educational support.' Pav said you'd – oh, good, here he is, hiya, just in the nick of –

PAV *comes in, taking off a motorbike helmet.*

PAV. Sorry, people – had to get Saff back to Amina, bendy bus jackknifed over three lanes, massive gridlock, what do they teach 'em, bus drivers?

NICK. Cycling proficiency. Assertiveness training.

RACHEL. We started without you.

PAV. Yeah, I see that.

RACHEL. Really need to start on the dot, we have a hell of a lot to get through before she gets here.

PAV. Yeah, okay, I think I just apologised –

LARA. Yes. I think he did.

NICK. We were just on 'providers'.

PAV. Cool. D'you circulate that stuff from Malmo, Nick?

NICK. From Malmo? Ah – did I get that? Shit.

RACHEL. Malmo? I certainly received nothing from Malmo or anywhere else.

PAV. Okay, give me a sec – on my phone, I can –

RACHEL. Sorry, but – what is this about?

LARA. Providers, subcontractors, of course.

PAV. Swedish educational outfit – based in Malmo.

NICK. By all accounts a sort of Swedish Portsmouth. Look, okay, I move that we put a couple of potential providers, such as our Swedes, in the appendix, and, Lara, you whack in a nominal consultancy fee – for Year One, because we can't really get into this now.

RACHEL. Oh. I think we seriously need to get into this now.

PAV. There you go. Okay. Banged over all the docs.

NICK. No, let's move to item three, and take that as read.

RACHEL. No, I'm still firmly on item two. Point of clarification needed.

NICK. Okay, Rach, this is, you're right, a big 'un, why don't we chat it over over glass of bubbly later –

RACHEL. No, I don't think so, I want this formally debated and minuted.

LARA. Sorry, Rachel, who's chairing this meeting?

NICK. Oh. Me, I think.

RACHEL. And who's Head Teacher of this school?

LARA. Nick's Head of Governors. Which actually trumps that.

PAV. Look, it's nothing heavy or – this outfit – they do consultancy, they set up systems, create curriculum stuff, they seed money – all run by ex-teachers, ex-inspectors – people basically like you.

RACHEL. Oh, so that's all right then?

NICK. So, thanks Pav, so – item three: admissions.

RACHEL. Look, I'm going to have to insist –

PAV. Yeah, but as clerk I have to say, technically you can't – insist.

RACHEL *looks at them, stunned. Then she gets up.*

RACHEL. Well, I can do this, can't I –

NICK. Do what?

RACHEL. Walk out. And how will your minutes look then?

Pause.

NICK. Okay. Five minutes on two and that's capped.

RACHEL *sits down*.

RACHEL. Thank you. So, let's go back a bit, so Pav, when you say 'outfit' you meant – ?

PAV. Well, yeah, a company, obviously –

RACHEL. Oh, right – like a profit-making, personal-enrichment sort of –

NICK. Rachel – come on –

RACHEL. Oh, is that really gauche of me? To ask that?

LARA. No comment.

PAV. Look, do you read the papers – every school's got private money all over it – buildings by Nord-Anglia –

NICK. Staffing courtesy of Serco –

LARA. School dinners from Burger King – ha!

RACHEL. But they don't run the whole damn show – if we get the green light after tonight, we'll get the per-pupil funding, just like any other school and I think, in that respect at least, we should be like any other school.

PAV. That's not the point. How do you think we're gonna pay for this place, getting it up to spec, getting in the best teachers? As ever, you're thinking way too small.

RACHEL. Am I? Am I really? That's interesting.

PAV. If we're part of a bigger entity with real capital in the bank, maybe we could meet all that demand here – meet it better. Set up one, two, maybe a chain of schools – I mean, even for a hundred, this is gonna be tight.

RACHEL. Ordinary schools manage all right.

PAV. We're not going to be a fucking ordinary school and we never were!

And don't, don't minute that. Sorry.

NICK. Rachel, this is very probably the future, firms like this, in partnership –

PAV. She can hardly say the public sector's good per se –

NICK. Pav, don't push it.

PAV. But if Government gets out of the picture, that's our
opportunity – right?

Pause.

RACHEL. Oh. Okay. Sorry, sorry – there seems to be quite a
consensus here – truly – look, have I been really dim, have
you been saying this all along or is this a new idea?

PAV. This was always the idea.

NICK. And it has to be said it works perfectly well for Eton and
Harrow.

LARA. They're charities. I expect we discussed this before
your time, Rachel. Before you got on board.

PAV. I mean, end of the day a school's just a service, right – just
delivering a service, like anything else, making PCs,
mobiles, operating a bank, a prison – right? And ten, fifteen
years from now, it's not gonna be 'send your child to the
one-size-fits-all school, courtesy of the Government' – I
mean, do you buy your clothes, your sounds, your house
from the Government?

RACHEL *laughs.*

RACHEL. Pav, I know we're in a shopping mall, but this is not
actually a shop –

LARA. Surely the real question is whether we want to be
Waitrose or Tesco –

PAV. Or Primark or TK Maxx, even – I guess the thing about
you teachers is you sort of see everything in black and white.

LARA. Teachers can be slightly... unworldly.

Pause. RACHEL *takes in their steadfastness;* NICK *won't
hold her gaze.*

RACHEL. Okay. Okay, Pav. Yes, you're right, this is a steep, a
vertical learning curve for me. My impulses, I guess, my
prejudices – oh, I can actually hear, right now, Dad, he was a

GP, unworldly too, railing against anything 'private', as if it was a toxin or – he'd blank a colleague who did even an hour's work privately – and, okay, I spent my childhood craving I dunno *Jackie* or even to watch ITV, for God's sake. 'No, no, no.' Maybe that's it, maybe I am made up of refusals – no to Live Aid, no to shares for BT or British Gas, no to – yes the same even for me as I worked – no to SATs, no to city technology colleges, no to academies, and every day, no to Tesco, no to *The X Factor* – yes, I'm pretty good at saying 'no' – I suppose – I suppose this is about saying 'yes' for once, right?

They're all looking at her.

NICK. Okay. Shall we simply put in that box that we are happy to forge partnerships with business and would welcome support from experienced educational providers? How would that sound?

PAV. That... sounds about right.

LARA. Fine by me.

RACHEL *shrugs*.

NICK. Item three: admissions.

RACHEL. Er, I'll speak to that.

LARA. Do we have time for this?

NICK. Three minutes precisely.

RACHEL. So we seem to be incredibly popular. Which is gratifying. And which means we have the luxury of choice; and the challenge of... that. We've said we want our school to have music-making at its heart. And we've had an incredible response to that notion. Which is, as I say, gratifying. But we have too many kids, too many. So, okay, how do we make the cut? We don't have an exam, rightly, we don't charge fees, of course, we need to take special-needs kids who nominate us and looked-after kids, as is only right, we are required to, to respond to our vicinity – loosely defined, but – but – here's the thing I suppose I'm starting to ask myself: did we get into this just to recreate The Mandela

– in terms of who comes through that door? Which, God, sounds… harsh – even as I say it. But – maybe our children should have to earn the right to come here – because whenever they don't, when it's there on a plate, won't they always hold what they have in contempt? I mean, I've seen that again and again, and this is absolutely not about background as such, this need not be about discriminating in any sense. So – okay, Nick, I know I'm – I would like to propose that when it comes to making the cut as to who comes to our school, musicality will be the key.

PAV. Which means exactly what?

RACHEL. Well. Off the top of my head, Grade One on an instrument of their choice, or they take a test of musical aptitude.

LARA. All the children?

RACHEL. Well, why not? They'll struggle without it. This is meant to be Concordia Academy – music at the heart of what we do, right.

NICK. So, okay, in the event of being oversubscribed, Grade One kids are prioritised from within the catchment?

RACHEL. Or those who take our test. Which in the end is not actually that much to ask, is it?

Pause

NICK. Brilliant! I mean, well, for myself I think it makes perfect sense.

LARA. Sorry. Not workable. Legally. Breaches the Admissions Code –

RACHEL. Oh, this would still abide by the Admissions Code, largely –

LARA. Sorry, 'largely' isn't good enough. I can't see any precedent for testing for more than fifteen per cent purely on musical aptitude – and I don't think we can ask them to play any instrument that implies any lessons or coaching or, so that's Grade One out –

RACHEL. The test would assume a very basic level of musical awareness –

LARA. Rachel, I'm not making this up, I'm reading the code now –

RACHEL. Then this is what we do differently – I mean, we're meant to be a free school, aren't we, meant to be distinctive, everybody wants us to be distinctive – and the other free schools make that about being, I dunno, a Sikh, Jewish, Muslim – which is pretty bloody exclusionary but never mind – music makes no judgements about what you believe, about who you are, it's class-blind colour-blind –

PAV. Yeah, right –

RACHEL. Don't we want children here who will thrive with us and won't we simply fail children who need more… who have, well, let's say more… challenges?

PAV. Oh, like poor kids, right?

RACHEL. No, Pav, no, not at all –

LARA. Anybody we exclude can challenge us, because they can inspect the minutes of the admissions process and there are legions of lawyers out there –

RACHEL. That's the thing. Every school excludes, just usually after the fact when it's too late, we're – simply compelling them to actively choose us –

PAV. Yeah, I have a bit of problem with this. Major problem, actually.

NICK. Really? Not some sort of religious injunction against music?

PAV. I'm sorry?

LARA. Nick!

RACHEL. You need to take that back, Nick.

PAV. No, it's cool, it's interesting to hear it.

NICK. I only meant – I just happen to know that some Muslims –

PAV. Oh, so you think I'm like Mullah Omar or something? You think I go round smashing up CDs and stuff?

NICK. I don't know, Pav. I know almost nothing about you.

PAV. Okay, here's one thing for you then, my Saff's not musical, okay. And I'm not – none of us are musical. In that way. I mean, she never wanted to take lessons or nothing. And they cost a bomb.

RACHEL. No, they don't 'cost a bomb', that's not true.

PAV. They cost a bomb when you're broke.

RACHEL. Oh, but in terms of what they're worth – let's not get into this –

PAV. Yeah, but it's all right for you lot, this, this is all second nature to you – like some kind of culture-vulture thing –

LARA. Pav, we don't all agree –

NICK. Anyway, we can hardly design the school around the needs of individual parents.

PAV. Oh right – but that's exactly what you're doing now, isn't it? This is Rachel's dream school. The school she didn't get first time round.

RACHEL. Pav, if we don't filter these applications in some way, we'll have a world of woe coming through that door – the addresses here, the names and addresses, I tell you, if they are our only pupils, we will have a majority of kids on free school meals, a majority of kids with English as an additional language, kids who need to be in care not in schools, traumatised, attention-deficit kids, and I have nothing but pity for those children but if they are anything more than a minority... I simply think we'll get nowhere.

PAV. Yeah, got you, Rachel, I know just what you mean – you're talking black kids, brown kids, immigrant kids? Am I right?

RACHEL. What? What did you say? Did I say anything, anything –

LARA. Pav, she didn't – she didn't say that – and you know she didn't –

PAV. Oh, nobody needs to say nothing, she knows what I mean, you know exactly what I mean, it's the dog-whistle thing, right, you know it when you hear it – you know what, fuck that, I am not going to be any part of any of that –

NICK. Pav, you might want to take that back. In fact, I insist you take it back.

PAV. No, fuck this, okay, fuck all this – white, middle-class – shit –

He's getting up.

Yeah, I know what you all think of me – just some pushy Paki on the make here, right – but say this, none of this was ever meant to be about freezing out poor kids, unlucky kids, far as I was concerned, it was meant to be about taking everyone with us, giving them the better stuff.

NICK. Yeah, we all know you have some colossal chip on your shoulder –

LARA. Nick, shut up –

PAV. Oh yeah, go on, Nick, always got some clever shit to say –

RACHEL. I was honestly only trying to be pragmatic – you seem, I dunno, you have seemed all along to have some issue with me –

PAV. You know you still don't remember me, do you, Miss De Witt – but you know what, I so remember you. Just the same, but older. Remember your voice, your perfume, your blouse, your nice shoes, but to you I'm just one more blurred brown face, right, just another little soul you didn't save.

PAV *walks out.*

RACHEL. What? I honestly have no idea what he's talking about?

LARA. Oh, apparently, apparently you taught him. Way back.

RACHEL. How could that be true? I mean, you teach hundreds of kids in your life, hundreds, you can't be expected to – shit.

NICK. Well, he was starting to get on my wick anyway –

LARA. Pav sourced this space, he did our website, he's worked flat out for nothing for six months and –

NICK. Well, why don't you trot after him and stroke his bruised ego or whatever else you fancy –

LARA. You – you are – you are completely –

LARA stands up. NICK goes over to her, she shoves him away awkwardly.

NICK. Lar – look –

LARA. Just – some sort of – minimal – respect – would be. Maybe too much to –

NICK receives a text.

NICK. I didn't – Lar – okay – it's her. Milly Molly Mandarin. Right. Fuck. She needs me to meet her and –

RACHEL. And what about Pav? Okay, I'll go and – ?

NICK. No, it's fine, we do this without him.

RACHEL. She thought we were borderline racists when we had him –

NICK. Who's the racist here, hey? Who has said anything at any point about race – ?

RACHEL. Yeah. Okay, okay. Oh. Look out for the kids. They'll be in uniform, Mandela uniform.

NICK goes. RACHEL and LARA alone. LARA checking her phone, close to tears.

Everything all right? With your –

LARA. Fine. Why shouldn't it be? Absolutely fine.

RACHEL. I'm sorry about that –

LARA. About what? Why would you be? You seem to be in complete agreement.

Pause.

RACHEL. Miranda okay?

LARA. Oh, Mirry's still not feeling too good. Why do you ask?

RACHEL. Been off a whole week now. Not had a doctor's note or –

LARA. Yes, as I say. There's something truly horrid going round. Children do tend to get ill, you don't have to take it personally.

RACHEL. Right, so not psychosomatic then?

LARA. What – why, why would it be fucking psychosomatic? What a catty thing to say.

Pause.

Okay, if you want the truth, she's not happy here, okay, so I'm keeping her off.

RACHEL. I see.

LARA. Because Miranda's a very special girl with very particular needs.

RACHEL. Well. All our children are –

LARA. And she gets bored very easily, she's just very bright, very attentive to atmosphere.

RACHEL. Okay. So she doesn't like the atmosphere –

LARA. And, Rachel, I have never believed in sacrificing my children to meet some, I dunno, ideological – whatever.

RACHEL. Oh, like me, you mean.

LARA. You said it, not me.

RACHEL. Okay. So where will she go now?

LARA. Well. I think we might be able to get her in to Latymer.

RACHEL. Okay. Congratulations. And does Nick know you're doing this?

LARA. Of course. Not that Nick's consent is a precondition of everything I do. And my patience with him is pretty much spent. You see, unlike you, I happen to live with him, I happen to sleep with him, I happen to breathe his air. And, I have to say, I'm starting to wonder whether that's good for either of us.

RACHEL. Well, I don't think we need a governor who doesn't believe in what I'm doing.

LARA. Rachel, it's you, you, it's all about you, isn't it, this? And sorry you can't sack governors, they sack you. I'm not in the mood for this. I need a drink. Oh, who bought that stupid bloody balloon?

LARA swipes the balloon aside as she goes. Alone, RACHEL tugs it down, looks at it.

MARTIN comes in. He watches her.

MARTIN. Something to celebrate?

RACHEL. Oh! Jesus.

MARTIN. Sorry. I would have knocked but I didn't see anything to knock.

Pause.

RACHEL. You're an hour late.

MARTIN. Sorry, I had to –

RACHEL. Every time you do that, and you do that every time you break his heart.

MARTIN. Yeah, there are reasons –

RACHEL. Such as the fact you're a shit father. You're a completely shit father.

MARTIN. Okay, okay. I'm sorry you think that. So where is he, then?

RACHEL. Oh, I don't know. Why would I know? I'm a shit mother.

MARTIN. Presumably he'll come back here. I can wait for him.

RACHEL. Actually, Martin, I'm in the middle of a very important meeting.

MARTIN. Right. What, governors' meeting?

RACHEL. Yes.

MARTIN. Well, maybe I'll sit here then.

RACHEL. In what capacity will you sit there?

MARTIN. Oh. Parent observer? What do you think?

RACHEL. Oh, shut up, shut up.

MARTIN. Naturally curious. As a parent. To see what the fuss is all about.

RACHEL. Look, Martin, if you've come all the way from Bicester just to dick about –

MARTIN. Oh, no, okay, I'm not in Bicester now.

Pause.

RACHEL. What? You're not in Bicester.

MARTIN. No, no – you'll be delighted to know it's not working, didn't work out, me, Nina, all that. No.

RACHEL. Why – why not? Why did it – ?

MARTIN. Oh. Well. In the end we, we didn't agree about very much. Which shouldn't matter, didn't matter initially –

RACHEL. Oh what, because you were shagging so much –

MARTIN. Oh, behave, Rachel –

RACHEL. And you, what, then you sated yourself on her and now you're –

MARTIN. 'Sated' myself? Sated myself? Jesus, your turn of phrase.

RACHEL. Now I almost feel sorry for her – you got your kicks –

MARTIN. Look, she threw me out last week. But, by last week, I think I wanted to go.

RACHEL. And why was that, what was the final straw?

MARTIN. Oh. Stupid things. It's cumulative, isn't it. Like, Nina doesn't read newspapers, oh no, but when she does she takes

The Times, and why does she take *The Times*, well, because
she considers *The Times* to be objective. *The Times*! Lots,
lots of stuff like that.

RACHEL. Oh dear.

Despite herself she laughs.

MARTIN. Yes, yes – you see, you understand. Oh, and get this,
Nina has a soft-top car, which I didn't mind, but what I
didn't like was the way she kept saying, endlessly, whenever
she went for a drive, 'It's just my personal little treat' – you
see my point? And of course she's too busy to watch films
but if she does watch telly, she generally opts for *Masterchef*
– at which, get this, she invariably cries.

RACHEL. While you make silly little cynical remarks –

MARTIN. Which very quickly started to grate on her, so much so
that I had to either sit in silence or walk the streets of Bicester,
which are surprisingly bloody bleak in midwinter. Oh, and all
of this might just have been sufferable until she 'fessed up to
having erotic dreams about – I kid you not – Nick Clegg.

RACHEL. Well, actually, I've always quite fancied Nick Clegg.

MARTIN. You do not – you cannot fancy Nick Clegg, he looks
like some fucking – gormless – teenage shop assistant in, in
where, in – River Island. No, no, he looks like the bass
guitarist in some Christian rock band – you do not fancy
Nick Clegg, Rachel!

RACHEL. So you found yourself arguing with your young
lover –

MARTIN. No, no, this, this was the worst of it – Nina flat
refuses to argue, if I challenge her, she will walk out of the
room, she accuses me of whingeing, she is the most ignorant,
expensively educated little – little –

RACHEL. Cow?

Pause.

MARTIN. Look, Rachel, what are you doing here? What are all
these lame adages, why on earth are you in this shop that

smells of trainers and general jock shit – I would dearly like to hear from you you're not seeing this through –

RACHEL. I don't want to hear this.

MARTIN. I know my shitty, my unforgiveable behaviour has driven you to throw in your lot with all this, that my midlife crisis has been contagious, and I am not saying you would ever think of taking me back –

RACHEL. Good, good, don't you ever think that –

MARTIN. Just tell me you're having cold feet, you're on the brink, with my help maybe, of walking away from this –

RACHEL. Oh no, oh no you don't, this is working, this is working well –

MARTIN. I know I have no right, I know I fucked up with you, I fucked up with Sam, I fucked up, okay, with the school – I know that – but what is this, Rachel? What is all this? Hey?

RACHEL. This is my life, is what it is, this, Martin, is what I can do without you.

He sits on the floor, rubs his face in his hands.

So I'd like you to go.

MARTIN. Threw myself on the mercy of Hammersmith and Fulham. Needless to say they weren't having any of it either, not least because they are having a love-fest with their Tory chums in Westminster where my job's now migrated.

RACHEL. Well, I'm obviously sorry to hear that, but I have to ask you leave.

MARTIN. What are the stats on single men in their forties on their own? I'm headed for penury and obesity.

RACHEL. Martin – you made your choice. And so did I.

MARTIN. Rachel. I want our life back and I'll do anything to get it.

NICK *re-enters with* POLLY.

NICK. This is the basic unit. I mean, obviously we are in the process of converting it, you can see traces of the former usage, still, but the current lessons take place in here – at the moment, it's just the pilot group, Rachel and some parent volunteers, but by September this will be fitted out, I can show you the architect's designs, but the walls will be one great music bar, staves, big treble clef here, and we're in talks with the LSO to partner on a number of fronts, but particularly in terms of musical equipment –

POLLY. I love your resourcefulness, this imaginative, innovative use of space, and also it's a sort of regeneration. Which I tell you ticks a box or two.

NICK. Oh yes, the neighbouring units are vacant, so very probably with the sort of demand –

POLLY. And interestingly enough, all the research shows that environment has very little bearing on learning – which I find kind of counterintuitive. Okay, it's quite cold but presumably that can be… sorted. Hi, Rachel.

NICK *sees* MARTIN.

RACHEL. Hi.

NICK. Sorry. Who's this?

RACHEL. Oh. This, this is –

MARTIN. Yeah, hi, I'm a parent. Hello.

POLLY. Great idea, bringing in prospective parents, presumably as part of a whole-community conversation – round up the stakeholders! – Hello –

MARTIN. Martin.

POLLY. Okay, Martin – I'm Polly Tyneham, DfE. And, oh, get you, champagne!

RACHEL. Nick thought –

NICK. Listen, mate, you'd be very welcome to pop back later –

MARTIN. Okay, you're Nick Orme.

NICK. Yes. You have the advantage of me.

RACHEL. Martin, please leave.

MARTIN. You look exactly like I imagined. Except with a bit more hair.

NICK. I'm sorry?

POLLY. Now, okay, if this is everyone, it might be useful for me to rehearse the process –

NICK. Is this that – your – Martin?

RACHEL *nods*.

I think Martin here might need to leave before we –

MARTIN. No thanks, Nick. I'm waiting for my son.

NICK. Come on, mate. This is actually a private –

MARTIN. 'Mate'? No, it doesn't come natural to you. And I thought the idea of all this was to be democratic, Nick. Enlisting the good people of Shepherd's Bush.

NICK. Sure, sure. Through appropriate process.

MARTIN. So, I'm well up for a bit of involvement.

POLLY. So tonight, Martin, is the last stage before we sign off on the business plan for Concordia – which, between us, and I so shouldn't say this but it's Friday and I can't resist, is looking – great – one or two gaps, okay, but – then with the Minister's blessing we sign off, release those budget streams to follow those pupils, and this school opens doors for business – and I think what the governors have set up is what –

NICK. A kind of conversation –

RACHEL. I suppose we can call it that –

NICK. – with local youngsters, young people.

POLLY. Brilliant. The young.

MARTIN. And also now – parents. A parent.

POLLY. Well, parents drive everything we do.

RACHEL. Yeah, I should declare an interest, Polly.

POLLY. Oh. Okay.

RACHEL. Martin here is my ex. I thought I should declare that, in case it becomes relevant.

MARTIN. But is that a problem? I mean, with the Big Society, and this is sort of, Polly, this is sort of – that –

POLLY. Oh, 'Big Society'? Definitely. This epitomises it.

MARTIN. So there's gonna be a bit of that going on – interests, vested sometimes, but, come on, get used to it! Philanthropic husband-and-wife teams, like Melissa and Bill, or that nice man Philip Green, brought in to kick ass –

POLLY. That's less Big Society, more –

MARTIN. 'Big Business', I know, but I just mean ordinary people who seek to do good but maybe also have an eye on the main chance – and all that's to be encouraged, right?

NICK. Jesus.

POLLY. We're certainly mad keen on – grass roots.

MARTIN. Exactly, grass roots, yeah, bottom-up, not like all that top-down, old-statist way, oh, that's gone, right out the window.

NICK. Polly, Martin here, in his slightly clichéd way, is striving to ironise –

POLLY. No, Nick, don't diss the parent – actually I think he's got a great grasp of –

MARTIN. Oh God, we can learn so much from business, the way business works, especially the finance sector, like the banking sector, so bring them in, bring on the bankers, sprinkle some of their stardust on the dowdy public sector.

NICK. Is this what passes for wit with you, Martin? Ben Elton circa 1982?

MARTIN. I'm actually quite flattered by that.

RACHEL. Well, just to say, in my view, if he had any consideration for my feelings he would leave, now.

MARTIN *sits down*.

NICK (*under his breath*). Prick.

POLLY. Where's all the others? Pav, was it?

RACHEL. Pav. Pav is –

NICK. Yes, Pav had to go home early – childcare I think – where's Lar?

RACHEL. I think Lara also had to deal with – something – pressing –

MARTIN. Childcare again?

NICK. Yeah. Yeah.

MARTIN. What these guys need are nannies-on-demand. Is that something they might get subsidies for, Polly, or maybe, what, tax breaks? Like in the old days, like wet nurses, the poor suckling and dandling the kids of the rich –

POLLY. Okay, look, I can't stop long, just want to say I am genuinely knocked out by what you have done – I mean, my God, look at this, this is amazing – there's a genuine, buzz, a genuine ambience that says something very special is happening here, about to happen here; and the work you have done on your plan is – awesome – I use that word too much, but really – and Michael, actually, really wanted me to convey to you, and not just Michael – all of us – we see you as, what, a pace-setter – I always get them mixed up with, pacemakers – pace-setter –

MARTIN. Okay, Nick, weren't you at Oxford or something with Michael Gove?

NICK. Is this your exposé moment? Sorry to disappoint you but I'd gone down before he came up. Apologies if that doesn't fit your *Weltanschauung*.

MARTIN. Nick, don't get all modest, mate, you were kicking around with them all, Boris, Michael, David, George – I can see you now, all gliding along in the same punt.

AMITHA, SADIE *and* MARCUS, *in uniform from The Mandela, come in. A moment. They dissolve into laughter.*

SADIE. I used to work in here – ohmygosh – this was SportsWorld.

AMITHA. Yeah, like ChavWorld, it was.

There's Miss. Hello, Miss.

RACHEL. Hi, great, come in, Mitha.

AMITHA. Oh – did I not tell you she would absolutely know my name?

MARCUS. Bet she don't know mine, though.

RACHEL. Course I do – Marcus. Thanks for coming.

SADIE. She knows mine.

RACHEL. Sadie.

SADIE. Respect, Miss.

NICK. Okay, Polly, so these, these young people are I think students taught previously by Rachel in the local school –

KIDS (*together*). Man-de-la – go, Man-de-la – go!!

NICK. That's, I guess, presumably ironic.

AMITHA. It's all right – you're all right. We're just a bit – y'know – mentalist.

SADIE. Friday night, innit.

RACHEL. Great, okay, guys. You know why you're here? Polly might want to tape some of this and take photos so there's a sort of consent, a sort of release form –

POLLY *is getting out a recorder.*

POLLY. I can do even better than that, I can record it.

RACHEL. And, basically, we just wanted to chat, to talk to you, to see how you would feel about what we're doing, planning.

POLLY. Oh, and I didn't – I'm Polly, I work for the Government. Say hi, so I can get a level.

AMITHA. Oh my days! You recording this for David Cameron?

POLLY. Well, not directly – him. So, Amitha, right.

AMITHA. David Cameron, I think you are well buff!

POLLY. I'm sure he'd be – hugely – flattered – and this is –

RACHEL. Marcus.

MARCUS. Now, I don't myself, personally, like you that much, David Cameron.

POLLY. Someone who might hear this, is the Secretary of State for Education, Michael Gove – now has anyone here heard of – ?

AMITHA. You cannot deny he is buff, Marcus.

SADIE. Gove? He's that one who's like a cute little boy?

AMITHA. Oh no, he is so freaky, man –

SADIE. Like Noddy or something – oh, I am sorry – that's actually quite rude.

POLLY. Okay, we can… we'll edit that out. Save his feelings.

Okay, Rachel.

RACHEL. Right, so, you know you're aware what's happening here? This place, this will be a free school, which is an entirely new sort of school.

SADIE. Oh yeah yeah yeah, I heard about this – this is weird –

POLLY. Great, great – that's actually quite encouraging that you have – what have you heard?

NICK. You could always stick your hand up. If you like. Then we could…

RACHEL. Nick. Don't be – wet.

NICK. Don't they stick their hands up these days?

MARTIN. Oh, it's all gone to cock, Nick – no standing up when Sir comes in, no payment by results, no birch, no fagging, teachers rarely wearing gowns.

AMITHA. School is free anyway. Like, personally, I don't pay no money for it.

RACHEL. No, not free in that sense, free from the control of –
local authorities –

AMITHA. What I do think is excellent, is like the thing about
the soldiers – like having some soldier taking PE – bare
muscles and –

MARCUS. Nah, they'd shout at you and dat. Do not approve a
that.

NICK. But, okay, would you say, would you say your
community might perhaps be keen to have a school
established such as this?

MARTIN. May I interject something?

NICK. No. No, you may not.

MARTIN. There's an interesting statistical pattern on this,
suggesting that what support there is, is non-existent with the
As, clusters in the B1s, tapers a little with Cs, and then
nosedives with Ds and Es.

RACHEL. How would you know? Did you do a phone survey
from Bicester?

POLLY. I'm keen to capture some more of the thoughts and
feelings of our young guests. Now, Rachel De Witt, I think
you used to teach these – students.

RACHEL. Oh yes. They're Year Ten.

SADIE. Year Eleven now, Miss, come on, Miss, keep up.

RACHEL. Okay, out of date. Sorry, and – Mitha. Okay, listen,
imagine this, imagine a school that started from scratch. That
could set its own class sizes, set its own rules, not copy the
failed, tired policies you saw through on day one, that could
devise its own curriculum shaped to the exact needs of the
students, not slog through something invented in their
absence, and that would have to shut up shop if it did not
deliver what it promised – that would be truly accountable. I
mean, you'd think that was a good idea, right? A completely
fresh start.

MARCUS. We was never told why you left.

AMITHA. I knew. Heard you was setting up this school thingy.

SADIE. All singing all day long, singing gay songs and shit.

AMITHA. Why's that gay? That's homophobic, anyway.

MARCUS. It's like not happening in here? Ah, that's fucked up –

RACHEL. Marcus –

NICK. You're not answering her question.

RACHEL. Nick.

NICK. Yes, she asked you to imagine an entirely different type of education.

SADIE. You know what, that's actually quite a cool idea, doing it here. It don't smell of school. Don't feel sick when you walk in, your heart sinks, mine does. You think here, this is part of what's round you. Not all set apart, like some prison. Everything grey, everything the same, depressing.

AMITHA. Get bored and you go to the nail bar or something.

NICK. That's it, guys, that's useful, it's useful to hear your thoughts about what you maybe don't get on with, in your current school –

MARTIN. Good stuff, Nick. Get them to pitch in. Rate-my-school-dot-com.

MARCUS. This guy cracks me up. He is bare random.

NICK. It would be really useful for the Minister to get a sense from the ground up as to what is wrong with current provision –

POLLY. Just to say this may not make it to the – to Michael.

MARTIN. Multiple-choice it: do you broadly welcome a new school in Shepherd's Bush? Strongly agree. Would you say present schools are serving the area to best effect? Strongly disagree. Do you think parents should have a larger say in –

RACHEL. We're not doing anything wrong here, in fact we're doing something that would never happen in any school I

have taught in, we're giving the students themselves the
chance to speak.

MARTIN. No, what it really is, guys, is these good people need
your school to be truly – trashed – basically because they
want to replace it, okay – because they want the money that
goes to it, which they think it doesn't deserve to have, am I
right? Polly?

POLLY. I think that's something of a major misrepresentation.

MARTIN. But in broad terms – so you need to really big up The
Mandela's problems, which could be tricky because largely
they're problems that are nothing to do with The Mandela,
about the catchment –

NICK. The soft bigotry of low expectations –

MARTIN. – problems these guys think can only be fixed by
starving it of cash –

RACHEL. That's the parents' choice not ours –

MARTIN. – basically making it worse and worse until it's
empty, until all the teachers drain away, all the kids boycott
it, except the truly most desperate ones, and then, then when
it's good and dead – I dunno, what then, Polly? Nick? Rach?

NICK. Look, you weren't invited here, I asked you not to
speak, now, now you're undermining what we're doing.

SADIE. Is that guy gonna be a teacher? I hate to be rude but I
don't think you'd be any good. At teaching and that.

RACHEL. Now look, listen to me, as you have come in here, as
you have come into this place – and it's really nice to see
you guys, actually –

AMITHA. Oh, Miss, I so used to like your lessons.

MARCUS. Yeah, we all liked her lessons. Her lessons were
bare live, man.

AMITHA. Like we sang really nice songs. I loved all that
singing, man. Those old songs, by Oasis and people.

RACHEL. Well, I know, I really liked the lessons too.

AMITHA. But, what, did you like get tired of us? Like – disrespecting you?

SADIE. Like, evidently – I would. Be real.

MARCUS. Oh, did we do something, like, bad to make you do this, Miss?

AMITHA. Yeah. All right, we were bad, but we weren't, like, nasty-bad –

RACHEL. Oh look, I think, I always thought you were terrific. But I could never – the way it's set out, the whole game – look, yes I am saying your school is not working. What have you got from it? What will you have? Marcus, you're on track for maybe one GCSE, if that, okay, so what was it for, all that time, eleven years in school, what can you even do with that, I mean – Amitha, when you came in, you shone with excitement, and you had to smother that light, didn't you, under a bushel, or Sadie, you too, in Year Seven, then it was relentless, sexualising you, you didn't have a chance to – come on, did it work for you? I don't like saying this. But you've been betrayed. And, okay, I was part of that betrayal. People like Martin – they talk the talk, great, The Mandela, but when push comes to shove they cross the street from it, they withhold their, our children. How can we let that continue? Because I have seen it continue for twenty years and I can't – I won't – y'know.

POLLY *switches off her tape.*

POLLY. I suspect we might want to call it a wrap there.

MARCUS. So how's this help us now? Like, if it was so bad, why didn't you –

RACHEL. I would so have loved you to have come to this school. I would so have loved this school to have been there for you. Truly if it were in my powers, you would come to this school, today, tomorrow, you would.

MARCUS. Yeah, right.

SADIE. Oh no, what's that stench? Gotta be Brandon.

AMITHA. Man, that boy smells bad.

RACHEL. Brandon?

BRANDON *slopes in, fiddling with an iPod.*

BRANDON. Hey, fuckers.

RACHEL. Okay, this is – this is Brandon.

AMITHA. Brandon's permanently excluded, Miss.

BRANDON. Happy day, happy day.

SADIE. You had a knife, you dick.

MARCUS. Smoked weed in ICT.

BRANDON. Who fucking care, man. What's all this shit?

NICK. Could you moderate your language?

BRANDON. Moderate your language, granddad.

RACHEL. Just, just ignore him, Nick.

POLLY. We were talking about free schools. Have you heard of them?

BRANDON. She's nice. Hello!

POLLY. I'm sorry, I don't think I asked you –

BRANDON. Free school, yeah, yeah, I know about it. That's where they gonna split us up, right, put all the black kids all together, yeah, all the white kids all together, all them Muslim kids all together, and all the Sikh kids all together, and the Jewish kids all together – I think that's sweet, that. I learn nothing with all them people. White with the white. Heavy.

MARTIN *laughs.*

MARTIN. He's brighter than he looks.

BRANDON. You fucking laughing at me?

POLLY. Was Brandon invited?

RACHEL. No, Brandon wasn't invited.

BRANDON. Marcus, man, see what I got. (*Brandishes the iPod.*) Nice one. Check it out. Later, people.

BRANDON *goes.*

MARCUS. Let's go, blood. This is bullshit this.

SADIE. All right – bye, Miss. Bye bye, Mrs Politician.

AMITHA. Hey, for the record, Miss – I'm gonna get five GCSEs. Picked up my act. Going to college and all that. Just for the record.

RACHEL. Well, I'm really really pleased to hear that. Really. Obviously.

AMITHA. See ya, Miss. You take care.

The schoolkids leave laughing and chanting 'Man-del-a, Man-del-a.'

POLLY. You tend to find – in these circumstances – a lot of confusion – but I think it might have been better set up. Perhaps.

NICK. Hardly helped by disinformation – flagrant prejudice – and the thing is, these kids are clearly not very bright.

MARTIN. They saw straight through you.

RACHEL. It was a mistake. I should never have brought those children here, I would never, I don't know – what was I thinking!

MARTIN. Yes, I have something I want to present. Just the three copies. One for the Head of Governors, Mr Orme here. One for yourself, Polly. One for you, Rachel.

NICK. No thanks.

POLLY. What is it?

MARTIN. Well, essentially what you have in there is a petition, signed by over a thousand local parents, and local teachers, former colleagues of yours, Rachel –

RACHEL. Right.

MARTIN. Jo Cheng started it. I think most of the teachers in the borough – some unions, of course, NUT, Unison, er –

NICK. Of course, the bloody unions.

MARTIN. – who else, Campaign for State Education –

NICK. Ah, backed by the SWP, I believe –

MARTIN. – basically we've assembled a case against your proposed school, which you can read, which basically boils down to questions of the appropriateness of the premises –

NICK. Not our old friend Health and Safety –

MARTIN. – basically suggesting this place violates various legs and regs –

NICK. Why not draw on the EU, perhaps – EU standards?

MARTIN. Yeah, we do –

NICK. Not forgetting all that lovely equality legislation?

MARTIN. Yep. That too.

NICK. God, you're pitiful. The poverty of your imagination.

Pause.

MARTIN. So, as I say, the petition, first, then the letter I drafted, which has all the, all the key points of the – there.

RACHEL, NICK *and* POLLY *look through the documents.*

No one knows quite what to do.

RACHEL. Why, why are you doing this, Martin? I mean, you have to agree, it's quite… personal. The manner in which you're… doing this.

MARTIN. I want our life back. I want to live in Shepherd's Bush with you. I want Sam to muddle his way through Mandela and for us to make that work for him. I want us to get off our knees, I want to fight for what we fought for, our parents fought for, I want to defend every benefit and every extra year of school and every free place at uni and every bit of social housing and every park and public holiday, all of the things that almost made the world a little more just, all those things they say we can't pay for, that we don't deserve, all the things they tell us don't belong to us – and this, all this is just a massive diversion from that – I want you to wake up – because, we faltered – but, Rach, we are the people we are for a reason –

POLLY. Okay. Thank you for your contribution. The truth of the matter is we consider this school will transform educational opportunities in this borough for all the children of this borough, that it provides a chance to give parents such as yourself a genuine choice and essentially I don't think this is likely to change our minds. The only certain thing about all of this is there is no way back from here. There are hundreds of groups of people signed up to establish free schools. Some might be stopped in their tracks; but that won't change the overall direction of travel. Right. Okay. Here we go! So. That was... that was good. Instructive. Ah, we didn't get to raise a glass. But we will. We absolutely will.

POLLY *goes*.

NICK. If I was a violent man I would do something extremely – violent – to you.

MARTIN. Last had a fight when I was twelve so the odds are in your favour.

NICK. Rachel, how did you ever end up with such a class-A arsehole?

RACHEL. Not now, Nick.

NICK. These people, they have no answers. All you know, the only thing you know is what went down before. Glued to the past like a dog to its puke, defending a broken settlement because you're up to your necks in it, yes, because you are its clients, feeding off it, indifferent as to whether it works or – and then you're low, dishonourable in your tactics, low and cheap and – you're parasites.

RACHEL. Nick, would you just fuck off, please!!

NICK. What?

RACHEL. Did you even notice your wife walked out on you? Does that not matter to you? You don't seem to notice things. Have you no idea what just happened? You haven't a clue what just happened. I don't blame you, I should have known what you are, I'm not blaming you for anything – but will you please just go away.

NICK. Okay. Okay. I will. Fine. Never forget, Rachel, you are worth twenty of him – and, okay, I may be a prat, I may fuck up, but I don't think you could claim I ever lied to you.

RACHEL. No. I don't think you did. Actually, I didn't need you to.

NICK goes. RACHEL and MARTIN alone. A long silence. The sounds of the street coming through. MARTIN fiddles with the champagne.

MARTIN. We get to drink this, then.

RACHEL. Nobody here deserves champagne.

MARTIN. Shame to waste it.

He looks at it. Puts it down.

RACHEL. You have absolutely no claim on me. None.

Pause.

MARTIN. I figure we're too old to play games. I reckon we need to own what we are now. Defend it.

RACHEL. Now I remember him! Parvez Akhtar. Wanted to be in the orchestra but he couldn't play for toffee, had no ear for it. Little bullied shrimp of a boy. Oh. He was a nice boy, but he simply had no ear… for music.

SAM comes in, looking dishevelled, with no iPod.

MARTIN. Hey! Hello, mate.

SAM says nothing.

Sorry I was late again and that. Unacceptable, I know.

But I'm here now, not going anywhere now.

And I think, you know what, I think we should all go out. Maybe go up the South Bank. Get some standbys. Have a pizza or maybe something Thai. What do you reckon? Sam?

SAM. Only if Mum comes.

MARTIN. Okay. I don't know, don't reckon your mum'd be up for that.

SAM. I'll come if she comes.

MARTIN. Yeah, but she may not want to come, Sam. What then?

SAM. Then you'll have to go on your own.

Pause.

MARTIN. What do you think, Rachel? What do you say to us heading over to the South Bank? Rachel?

RACHEL *looks at them as if she doesn't recognise them.* SAM *holds the balloon.*

SAM. Mum, Brandon nicked my iPod.

RACHEL. Sam – oh, Sam –

She embraces SAM. *He lets her.* MARTIN *watches them.*

I don't know what you think, but I think society is like this great, big wound. With no boundaries to it. With the skin, breaking in all directions. And each torn tissue connected to each torn tissue. And however much you attempt, maybe to sew or to staunch or to bandage it, the wound weeps, it weeps and all you can do is keep the pressure, keep the lint on the wound and keep the pressure on and if you once take the pressure off, I don't know… and are we qualified to – do we have it within us – do we even have the will – but it's our wound, the wound is a wound to our bodies too, so we really have no choice, no choice at all but to keep the pressure on.

I don't know, that's just suddenly how I see it.

Blackout.

The End.

A Nick Hern Book

Little Platoons first published in Great Britain in 2011 as a paperback original by Nick Hern Books Limited, 14 Larden Road, London W3 7ST, in association with the Bush Theatre, London

Little Platoons copyright © 2011 Steve Waters

Steve Waters has asserted his moral right to be identified as the author of this work

Cover image by aka; photograph by Graham Michael
Cover design by Ned Hoste, 2H

Typeset by Nick Hern Books, London
Printed in the UK by CLE Print Ltd, St Ives, Cambs PE27 3LE

A CIP catalogue record for this book is available from the British Library

ISBN   978 1 84842 151 6

Amateur Performing Rights   Applications for performance, including readings and excerpts, by amateurs in English throughout the world should be addressed to the Performing Rights Manager, Nick Hern Books, 14 Larden Road, London W3 7ST, *tel* +44 (0)20 8749 4953, *fax* +44 (0)20 8735 0250, *e-mail* info@nickhernbooks.demon.co.uk, except as follows:

Australia: Dominie Drama, 8 Cross Street, Brookvale 2100, *fax* (2) 9938 8695, *e-mail* drama@dominie.com.au

New Zealand: Play Bureau, PO Box 420, New Plymouth, *fax* (6)753 2150, *e-mail* play.bureau.nz@xtra.co.nz

South Africa: DALRO (pty) Ltd, PO Box 31627, 2017 Braamfontein, *tel* (11) 712 8000, *fax* (11) 403 9094, *e-mail* theatricals@dalro.co.za

United States of America and Canada: Micheline Steinberg Associates, see details below

Professional Performing Rights   Application for performance by professionals in any medium and in any language throughout the world (and for amateur and stock performances in the USA and Canada) should be addressed to Micheline Steinberg Associates, 104 Great Portland Street, London W1W 6PE, *tel* +44 (0)20 7631 1310, *e-mail* info@steinplays.com

No performance of any kind may be given unless a licence has been obtained. Applications should be made before rehearsals begin. Publication of this play does not necessarily indicate its availability for amateur performance.